Listen and

Spanish

BY FRANK THOMPSON

Professor of Spanish

New York University

and

The Editorial Staff of

DOVER PUBLICATIONS, INC.

DOVER PUBLICATIONS, INC.
NEW YORK

Published in Canada by General Publishing Company, Ltd., 30 Lesmill Road, Don Mills, Toronto, Ontario.

Published in the United Kingdom by Constable and Company, Ltd., 10 Orange Street, London WC 2.

Standard Book Number: 486-20876-1
Library of Congress Catalog Card Number: R60-112

Manufactured in the United States of America
Dover Publications, Inc.
180 Varick Street
New York, N. Y. 10014

CONTENTS

	Page	Side	Band
Introduction	5		
Pronunciation	15		
Spanish Alphabet . . .	18		
Greetings, Introductions and Social Conversation	19	1	1
Yourself	22	1	2
Making Yourself Understood .	24	1	2
Useful Words and Expressions .	26	1	3
Difficulties	29	1	4
Customs	30	1	5
Baggage	32	1	5
Travel: General Expressions . .	33	2	1
Tickets	36	2	2
Boat	38	2	2
Airplane	39	2	2
Train	40	2	3
Bus and Streetcar . .	41	2	3
Taxi	42	2	3
Automobile Travel . .	43	2	4
Parts of the Car . .	45	2	4
At the Hotel . . .	47	3	1
At the Café . . .	52	3	2
At the Restaurant . .	53	3	3
Food List . . .	57	3	3
Breakfast Foods . .	59	4	1
Soups and Entrées . .	60	4	1
Vegetables and Salad . .	62	4	1
Fruits	64	4	1
Beverages . . .	65	4	1

4　　　　　　　　　　　**CONTENTS**

	Page	Side	Band
Desserts	65	4	1
At the Restaurant (Conversation)	66	4	1
Church	69	4	2
Sightseeing	69	4	2
Amusements	70	4	3
Sports	72	4	3
Bank and Money	73	5	1
Shopping	74	5	2
Shopping List	76	5	2
Colors	80	5	2
Stores	82	5	2
Bookstore and Stationer's	83	5	3
Cigar Store	85	5	3
Camera Shop	86	5	4
Drugstore	87	5	4
Laundry and Dry Cleaning	90	6	1
Barber Shop and Beauty Parlor	91	6	1
Health and Illness	92	6	2
Dentist	94	6	2
Telephoning	95	6	3
At the Post Office (Conversation)	96	6	3
Sending a Telegram (Conversation)	97	6	3
Time and Time Expressions	99	6	4
Days of the Week	101	6	4
Months and Seasons	101	6	4
Weather	103	6	4
Numbers	104	6	5
Signs and Public Notices	106		
Road Signs	112		
Native Food and Drink List	115		
Index	127		

INTRODUCTION

The Plan and Presentation of "Listen and Learn"

Listen and Learn Spanish is an introductory course designed to give you the basic sentences, phrases, and vocabulary that you will need in almost every travel situation. The course does not pretend to teach the grammatical structure of Spanish through a series of progressive and graded lessons. You will, however, absorb much of the structure of the language in the unconscious way you first learned English as a child. You need not start at the beginning; listen and learn whatever sections interest you. Although a systematic study is probably most desirable, don't feel obliged to master any series of phrases before going on to the next. This course differs from many others in that whatever you learn will be useful regardless of your previous study, your rate of forgetting, your length of study.

You will observe that *Listen and Learn Spanish* is a straightforward course designed to help you solve real travel problems. Its value rests as much on what is omitted as on what is included. You will find "Give me small change" (an urgent need in foreign travel), but do not look for "This is the pen of my aunt."

Listen and Learn Spanish teaches you what *you* will say, not what you will hear. This plan is a deliberate editorial policy based on travel experience. No editor can possibly anticipate the exact form in which your question will be answered. A waiter can be anything from taciturn to over-talkative. He may answer your question by a silent nod or by voluble news of his cousin in Toledo. The editors have, therefore, framed most questions and statements to elicit a simple response that will probably contain the very words in your question.

The section on making yourself understood (entries 50 to 64) will come to your aid in achieving comprehension. Phrases such as "Please speak more slowly," "I speak a little Spanish," are essential because the reasonably good pronunciation you will achieve through imitation will often suggest a greater mastery of the language than you may actually have.

Suggested Method for Study—The Records

In the recordings, each phrase is spoken in English and in Spanish followed by a pause sufficient to allow for repetition.* After some practice, you may wish to use this pause to anticipate the next phrase and check your pronunciation against that of the speaker. If you first listen to the records while following the text you will find the separate study of record and text more meaningful. Play the records whenever you have an opportunity, while working, engaging in a hobby—whenever you are within listening range of a record player. Although active participation is best, even passive but repeated listening will familiarize you with useful Spanish.

---

* Except for three brief sections of dialogue, presented at the normal rate of delivery in order to acquaint you with the rhythm and flow of Spanish in ordinary conversation. These sections are noted in the table of contents, and in the recordings each begins with a warning that dialogue follows.

Suggested Method for Study—The Manual

The *Listen and Learn Spanish* manual is complete in itself and is designed so that you can carry it in your pocket for unobtrusive reference and study. Read it at odd moments—while commuting, eating, waiting —and try to learn 10 or 15 phrases a day and test your pronunciation against the records later. In 30 to 60 days, you will know the language essential for travel.

Of course, you will take the manual with you when you go abroad. All that you have learned will be available to you for reference and refresher study.

You will find the extensive index on pages 127–140 especially helpful. Notice that each entry in the book is numbered and that the index refers to these numbers. The indexing method enables you to locate information quickly and without searching the whole page.

Use the index to test yourself. It contains every important word and phrase that you have learned in the *Listen and Learn Spanish* course. Test your vocabulary and your ability to form phrases and questions from the words in the index.

The manual is designed to help you form additional sentences of your own. For the words in square brackets you can substitute the words immediately following (in the same sentence or in the indented entries below). For example, the entry

I am [hungry] thirsty.

provides two sentences: "I am hungry" and "I am thirsty." Three sentences are provided by the entry

I am a [student].
—— teacher.
—— businessman.

As your Spanish vocabulary increases, you will find that you can express a wide range of thoughts by substituting the proper words in these type-sentences.

Parentheses are used in the manual to indicate words that may or may not be wanted in a sentence; example

I (do not) understand.

Speak Spanish When You Travel

When you travel abroad, do not be timid about using what you have learned. The native listener is always pleased and flattered when you attempt to speak his language. Whether this is your first trip or your twenty-first, your native listener will know that you are an American (years of intensive study will never disguise this fact), and he is ready to accept pronunciation and grammar less than perfect. So do not be self-conscious if your speech is halting and awkward. Speak politely, boldly, and clearly. Timid mumbling may be a greater barrier to comprehension than faulty pronunciation. Remember, your purpose is to communicate, not to pass as a native of Spain or Latin America.

The *Listen and Learn Spanish* course will enable you to communicate on a simple but very practical level. You will make yourself understood in everyday matters. With time and further study, improvement will come and the range of your conversation will expand. Do not, however, let your present inability to discuss Spanish novels or the current political scene inhibit you from asking questions in Spanish. You know your own language limitations, and you must speak Spanish within and in spite of them.

Bear in mind that your Spanish listener is not judging or grading you. He is kindly disposed towards you and is especially interested in trying to communicate. When you succeed in making yourself understood in Spanish you will have achieved your aim. If you are interested in a grade, score yourself 100%.

Speak the Spanish you have learned from *Listen and Learn Spanish*. The effort will not only make your travel more exciting and rewarding but will also contribute to better foreign relations. Too many Americans who travel demand that all peoples of the world speak English—an attitude that non-Americans find narrow and condescending. If you are willing to meet and speak to people in their own language, you may not impress them with your command of the subjunctive, but you will create an impression more representative of the warmth, open-mindedness, and democratic feeling of America. This impression may be more valuable than thousands of words of propaganda.

FOR FURTHER STUDY

After you have mastered the material of *Listen and Learn Spanish* you may wish to continue with more formal study in order to become more fluent in speaking, reading, and writing. It is entirely possible to carry on study by yourself with a few well-selected books and with such audio-visual material aids as Spanish movies, newspapers, records, etc.

The following books can be purchased through your local dealer for the publisher's current (1982) list price.

Dictionaries

University of Chicago Spanish-English, English-Spanish Dictionary. Edited by Carlos Castillo and Otto F. Bond. Pocket Books, 630 Fifth Avenue, New York, N.Y. 10020. 544pp. $2.95 pocket size. You will do well to purchase this book or another pocket dictionary immediately.

A Phrase and Sentence Dictionary of Spoken Spanish, prepared by U. S. War Dept., Dover Publications, Inc., $5.95. Contains phrases, sentences, words in context.

Introductory Grammars

Español en Directo, by Sánchez et al., has two textbooks for the first two levels of Spanish (1A and 1B). Textbooks are $9.50 each, and workbooks are also available, at $5.95. Published by SGEL, SA in Madrid, Spain, and available from The French & Spanish Book Co. (see p. 13 for address) .

Spanish Grammar, by Eric V. Greenfield. Barnes & Noble, 105 Fifth Avenue, New York, N.Y. 236pp. $3.95. Most useful for those with some prior study of Spanish.

Readers

Graded Spanish Reader, ed. by Manuel Durán, D. C. Heath & Co., 125 Spring St., Lexington, Mass. 02173. $6.95.

Panorama: Lecturas Primeras by Zenia S. Da-Silva, Harper & Row, 144pp. $8.95.

Novels and general literature

Your local dealer probably has a small selection of foreign-language books, but a visit there may be rewarding. The following specialist dealers have larger stocks ranging from elementary to advanced levels. Some will send you catalogues and announcements if you drop them a card.

Kroch's and Brentano's, 29 South Wabash Avenue, Chicago, Ill. 60603.

R. H. Macy's Book Department, Herald Square, New York, N.Y. 10001.

Adler's Foreign Books, 162 Fifth Avenue, New York, N.Y. 10010.

Barnes and Noble, Inc., 105 Fifth Avenue, New York, N.Y. 10003.

The French and Spanish Book Co., 115 5th Ave., New York, N.Y. 10003.

Schoenhof's Foreign Books, Inc., 1280 Massachusetts Avenue, Cambridge, Mass. 02138.

Stechert-Hafner, Inc., 866 Third Avenue, New York, N.Y. 10022.

Las Américas Publishing Co., 52 East 23rd Street, New York, N.Y. 10010.

The following publishers have an extensive list of foreign language books and will supply their catalogs upon request.

Appleton-Century-Crofts, Inc., 292 Madison Avenue, New York, N.Y. 10017.

D. C. Heath and Co., 125 Spring Street, Lexington, Mass. 02173.

Oxford University Press, 200 Madison Avenue, New York, N.Y. 10016.

University of Chicago Press, 5801 Ellis Avenue, Chicago, Ill. 60637.

Spanish Periodicals

To develop your comprehension the following publications are recommended. Of course, they require a more advanced grasp of Spanish, and you would do well to first buy an individual issue to determine whether the material is within your reading ability.

La Prensa, 181 Hudson St., New York, N.Y. 10013. $0.30 daily, $0.50 Sunday, $98.00 for one year.

Selecciones del Reader's Digest, Pleasantville, N.Y. 10570, publishes monthly selections of its articles translated into Spanish. $16.93 per year in the United States.

Spanish radio and television programs

Broadcasts in Spanish provide a variety of intonation, expression, and subject matter, and thus offer an excellent means of quickening your comprehension. Spanish language programs are offered by more than 150 stations in the United States. Your local paper is the best source of current information.

The Voice of America broadcasts over the network of 78 transmitters, around the clock and around the globe. The U. S. Information Agency, Washington, D.C. 20525, will send full details on these programs.

PRONUNCIATION

Listen and Learn Spanish is based upon Latin-American usage. There are variations in pronunciation, vocabulary and phrasing in different countries and regions. These variations, however, are not great enough to affect correctness or comprehension in the Spanish-speaking world.

The simplified phonetic transcription is given as an aid to correct pronunciation. The transcription should be read as though it were English. Stressed syllables are printed in capital letters. The rules of Spanish pronunciation are not difficult and their application is regular. **It is not necessary to memorize these rules in order to benefit from the records** although it is helpful to note those letters which have a different pronunciation in Spanish as indicated by the notes in the table which follows. The best guide is listening to native speakers and attempting careful imitation.

In the phonetic system, consistency is sometimes sacrificed for simplicity and ease of comprehension. You are urged to use it only as a temporary guide; abandon it as soon as possible. If you study Spanish in a class or with a private teacher, the teacher may ask you to drop it so as to avoid confusion with other systems.

There are no sounds in Spanish that cannot be pronounced with ease by the average American. The main difference between Spanish and English speech is in the pronunciation of the vowels. In Spanish, the vowels are pure sounds, not diphthongs as in English. Try to pronounce the sound of *ay* (as in s*ay*) without permitting yourself to end on the sound of *ee*. Similarly, pronounce *oh* without ending on the sound of *oo*.

The combinations SYOHN, KYAY, TYAY, LYAH, etc., are pronounced as single syllables in which the *y* is pronounced as a consonant, as in *y*es.

SCHEME OF PRONUNCIATION

Letter	Transcription	Example	Notes
a	ah	as in father	
b	b	as in boy	
c	s or k	as in say or kite	c is pronounced like s before e and i; like k before all other vowels and consonants.
ch	ch	as in church	
d	d	as in day	
e	e or ay	as in met or daytime	
f	f	as in fall	
g	g or h	as in go or hold	g is pronounced like h before e and i; before all other vowels and consonants it is hard, as in go.
h	—	silent	
i	ee	as in feel	
j	h	as in hold	
l	l	as in let	
ll	y	as in yes	

Letter	Transcription	Example	Notes
m	m	as in *m*et	
n	n	as in *n*ot	
ñ	ny	as in ca*ny*on	
o	o or oh	as in n*o*te	
p	p	as in *p*ay	
q	k	as in *k*ite	
r	r	as in *r*ed	Roll the *r* with the tip of the tongue.
rr	rr	as in *r*ed	More strongly trilled than a single *r*.
s	s	as in *s*ay	
t	t	as in *t*ell	
u	oo	as in f*oo*d	
v	v	as in *v*ase	
x	ks	as in pic*ks*	
y	ee	as in f*ee*l	
z	s	as in *s*ay	

Note: *hay* has been transcribed as *I* in " I am " and *ai* has been transcribed as *ie* in " lie ".

THE SPANISH ALPHABET

(not recorded)

The Spanish Alphabet is given below along with the pronunciation of each letter according to this manual's transcription. You will find it useful in spelling out names and addresses.

Letter	Called	Letter	Called
A	ah	N	EN-ay
B	bay	Ñ	EN-yay
C	say	O	oh
CH	chay	P	pay
D	day	Q	koo
E	ay	R	ER-ay
F	EF-ay	RR	ER-ray
G	gay	S	ES-ay
H	AH-chay	T	tay
I	ee	U	oo
J	HO-tah	V	vay
K	kah	W	DAH-vay
L	el	X	AY-kees
LL	EL-yay	Y	ee gree-YAY-gah
M	EM-ay	Z	ZAY-tah

GREETINGS, INTRODUCTIONS AND SOCIAL CONVERSATION

SIDE ONE—BAND I

1. Good morning.
Buenos días.
BWAY-nohss DEE-ahss.

2. Good evening.
Buenas noches.
BWAY-nahss NO-chess.

3. Good-bye.
Adiós.
ah-DYOHSS.

4. Until next time.
Hasta la vista.
AHSS-tah lah VEESS-tah.

5. I wish to make an appointment with [Mr. Gonzáles].
Quiero hacer una cita con [el señor González].
KYAY-ro ah-SAYR OO-nah SEE-tah kohn [el say-NYOR gohn-SAH-less].

6. May I introduce [Mr., Mrs., Miss Garcia].
Permítame presentar [al señor, a la señora, a la señorita García].
payr-MEE-tah-may pray-sen-TAHR [ahl say-NYOR, ah lah say-NYOH-rah, ah la say-nyoh-REE-tah gar-SEE-ah].

7. —— my wife.
mi esposa.
mee ess-PO-sah.

8. —— my husband.
mi esposo.
mee ess-PO-so.

19

9. —— **my daughter.**
   mi hija.
   mee EE-hah.

10. —— **my son.**
    mi hijo.
    mee EE-ho.

11. —— **my friend.**
    mi amigo (*masc.*).
    mee ah-MEE-go.

12. —— **my sister.**
    mi hermana.
    mee ayr-MAH-nah.

13. —— **my brother.**
    mi hermano.
    mee ayr-MAH-no.

14. —— **my mother.**
    mi madre.
    mee MAH-dray.

15. —— **my father.**
    mi padre.
    mee PAH-dray.

16. —— **my child.**
    mi hijo (*masc.*).
    mee EE-ho.

17. **I am glad to meet you.**
    Me alegro de conocerle.
    may ah-LAY-gro day ko-no-SAYR-lay.

18. **How are you?**
    ¿Cómo está usted?
    KO-mo ess-TAH oos-TED?

19. Fine, thanks. And you?
Muy bien, gracias. ¿Y usted?
mwee byen, GRAH-syahss. ee oos-TED?

20. How are things?
¿Qué tal?
kay tahl?

21. All right.
Bien.
byen.

22. So, so.
Así, así.
ah-SEE, ah-SEE.

23. How is your family?
¿Cómo está su familia?
KO-mo ess-TAH soo fah-MEE-lyah?

24. Very well.
Muy bien.
mwee byen.

25. Please sit down.
Haga el favor de sentarse.
AH-gah el fah-VOR day sen-TAHR-say.

26. I have enjoyed myself very much.
Me he divertido mucho.
may ay dee-vayr-TEE-doh MOO-cho.

27. Give my regards to your aunt and uncle.
Dé mis recuerdos a sus tíos.
day meess ray-KWAYR-dohss ah sooss TEE-ohss.

28. Come to see us.
Venga a vernos.
VEN-gah ah VAYR-nohss.

29. Give me your address and telephone number.
Déme su dirección y su número de teléfono.
DAY-may soo dee-rek-SYOHN ee soo NOO-may-roh day tay-LAY-fo-no.

30. May I call on you again?
¿Me permite visitarle otra vez?
may payr-MEE-tay vee-see-TAHR-lay O-trah vess?

31. I like you very much.
Me simpatiza mucho.
may seem-pah-TEE-sah MOO-cho.

32. Congratulations.
Felicitaciones.
fay-lee-see-tah-SYOH-ness.

33. Happy birthday.
Feliz cumpleaños.
fay-LEESS coom-play-AHN-yohss.

34. Happy New Year.
Feliz año nuevo.
fay-LEESS AHN-yo NWAY-vo.

35. Merry Christmas.
Feliz Navidad.
fay-LEESS nah-vee-DAHD.

YOURSELF

SIDE ONE—BAND 2

36. My name is [John].
Me llamo [Juan].
may YAH-mo [hwahn].

37. I am an American citizen.
Soy ciudadano americano.
soy syoo-dah-DAH-no ah-may-ree-KAH-no.

38. My mailing address is 920 Broadway.
Mi dirección para cartas es novecientos veinte
    Broadway.
mee   dee-rek-SYOHN   PAH-rah   KAHR-tahss   ess
    no-vay-SYEN-tohss VAYN-tay Broadway.

39. I am a [student].
Soy [estudiante].
soy [ess-too-DYAHN-tay].

40. —— teacher.
    profesor *(masc.)*.
    pro-feh-SSOR.

41. —— business man.
    hombre de negocios.
    OHM-bray day nay-GO-ssyohs.

42. I am a friend of Robert's.
Soy un amigo de Roberto.
soy oon ah-MEE-go day ro-BAYR-toh.

43. I am here on [a business trip] a vacation.
Estoy aquí [de negocios] de vacaciones.
ess-TOY ah-KEE [day nay-GO-see-ohss] day vah-kah-
    SYOH-ness.

44. We are traveling to Barcelona.
Viajamos a Barcelona.
vyah-HAH-mohss ah bahr-say-LO-nah.

45. I am in a hurry.
Tengo prisa.
TEN-go PREE-sah.

46. I am [hungry] thirsty.
Tengo [hambre] sed.
TEN-go [AHM-bray] sed.

47. I am [warm] cold.
Tengo [calor] frío.
TEN-go [kah-LOHR] FREE-o.

48. I am glad.
Me alegro.
may ah-LAY-gro.

49. I am sorry.
Lo siento.
lo SYEN-toh.

MAKING YOURSELF UNDERSTOOD

50. Do you speak English?
¿Habla usted inglés?
AH-blah oos-TED een-GLAYSS?

51. Does anyone here speak English?
¿Hay alguien aquí que hable inglés?
I AHL-gyen ah-KEE kay AH-blay een-GLAYSS?

52. I speak only English.
Sólo hablo inglés.
SO-lo AH-blo een-GLAYSS.

53. I speak a little Spanish.
Hablo un poco de español.
AH-blo oon PO-ko day ess-pah-NYOHL.

54. Please speak more slowly.
Favor de hablar más despacio.
fah-VOR day ah-BLAHR mahss dess-PAH-syoh.

55. I (do not) understand.
(No) comprendo.
(no) kohm-PREN-doh.

56. Do you understand me?
¿Me comprende?
may kohm-PREN-day?

57. I (do not) know.
(No) se.
(no) say.

58. I think so.
Creo que sí.
KRAY-oh kay see.

59. Repeat it, please.
Favor de repetirlo.
fah-VOR day rray-pay-TEER-lo.

60. Write it down, please.
Escríbalo, por favor.
ess-KREE-bah-lo, por fah-VOR.

61. What does this word mean?
¿Qué quiere decir esta palabra?
kay KYAY-ray day-SEER ESS-tah pah-LAH-brah?

62. What is that?
¿Qué es eso?
kay ess AY-so?

63. How do you say "match" in Spanish?
¿Cómo se dice "match" en español?
KO-mo say DEE-say "match" en ess-pah-NYOHL?

64. How do you spell "paella"?
¿Cómo se deletrea "paella"?
KO-mo say day-lay-TRAY-ah pah-AY-ah?

USEFUL WORDS AND EXPRESSIONS

SIDE ONE—BAND 3

65. Yes.
Sí.
see.

66. No.
No.
no.

67. Perhaps.
Puede ser.
PWAY-day sayr.

68. Excuse me.
Dispénseme.
deess-PEN-say-may.

69. Thanks (very much).
(Muchas) gracias.
(MOO-chahss) GRAH-syahss.

70. You are welcome.
No hay de que.
no I day kay.

71. It is all right.
Está bien.
ess-TAH byen.

72. It doesn't matter.
No importa.
no eem-POR-tah.

73. That is all.
Eso es todo.
AY-so ess TOH-doh.

74. Who are you?
   ¿Quién es usted?
   kyen ess oos-TED?

75. Who is [that boy]?
   ¿Quién es [ese muchacho]?
   kyen ess [ESS-ay moo-CHAH-cho]?

76. —— that girl.
   esa muchacha.
   ESS-ah moo-CHAH-chah.

77. —— that man.
   ese hombre.
   ESS-ay OHM-bray.

78. —— that woman.
   esa mujer.
   ESS-ah moo-HAYR.

79. Where is [the men's room]?
   ¿Dónde está [el cuarto de caballeros]?
   DOHN-day ess-TAH [el KWAR-toh day kah-bah-YAY-rohss]?

80. —— the ladies' room.
   el cuarto de damas.
   el KWAR-toh day DAH-mahss.

81. Who?
   ¿Quién?
   kyen?

82. What?
   ¿Qué?
   kay?

83. Why?
   ¿Por qué?
   por kay?

84. When?
¿Cuándo?
KWAHN-doh?

85. Where?
¿Dónde?
DOHN-day?

86. How?
¿Cómo?
KO-mo?

87. How much?
¿Cuánto?
KWAHN-toh?

88. How long?
¿Cuánto tiempo?
KWAHN-toh TYEM-po?

89. What do you wish?
¿Qué desea usted?
kay day-SAY-ah oos-TED?

90. Come here.
Venga acá.
VEN-gah ah-KAH.

91. Come in.
Pase usted.
PAH-say oos-TED.

92. Wait a moment.
Espere un momento.
ess-PAY-ray oon mo-MEN-toh.

93. Listen.
Oiga.
OY-gah.

94. Look out!
¡Cuidado!
kwee-DAH-doh!

DIFFICULTIES

SIDE ONE—BAND 4

95. Can you [help me] tell me?
¿Puede usted [ayudarme] decirme?
*PWAY-day oos-TED [ah-yoo-DAHR-may] day-
SEER-may?*

96. I am looking for my friends.
Busco a mis amigos.
BOOS-ko ah meess ah-MEE-gohss.

97. I cannot find my hotel address.
No puedo hallar la dirección de mi hotel.
*no PWAY-doh ah-YAHR lah dee-rek-SYOHN day mee
o-TEL.*

98. I lost [my purse] my wallet.
No encuentro [mi bolsa] mi cartera.
no en-KWEN-tro [mee BOHL-sah] mee kahr-TAY-rah.

99. I forgot my money.
Olvidé mi dinero.
ohl-vee-DAY mee dee-NAY-ro.

100. I have missed my train.
He perdido mi tren.
ay payr-DEE-doh mee tren.

101. What am I to do?
¿Qué debo hacer?
kay DAY-bo ah-SAYR?

102. My eyeglasses are broken.
Mis gafas están rotas.
meess GAH-fahs ess-TAHN RO-tahss.

103. Can you repair these shoes?
    ¿Puede componerme estos zapatos?
    PWAY-day kom-po-NAYR-may ESS-tohs sah-PAH-tohss?

104. The lost and found desk.
    La sección de objetos perdidos.
    lah sek-SYOHN day ohb-HAY-tohss payr-DEE-dohss.

105. The police station.
    La estación de policía.
    lah ess-tah-SYOHN day po-lee-SEE-ah.

106. I will call a policeman.
    Llamaré un policía.
    yah-mah-RAY oon po-lee-SEE-ah.

107. The American consulate.
    El consulado americano.
    el kohn-soo-LAH-doh ah-may-ree-KAH-no.

CUSTOMS

SIDE ONE—BAND 5

108. Where is the customs?
    ¿Dónde está la aduana?
    DOHN-day ess-TAH lah ah-DWAH-nah?

109. Here is [my baggage].
    Aquí está [mi equipaje].
    ah-KEE ess-TAH [mee ay-kee-PAH-hay].

110. —— my passport.
    mi pasaporte.
    mee pah-sah-POR-tay.

111. —— my identification papers.
    mi carnet de identificación.
    mee kahr-NAY day ee-den-tee-fee-kah-SYOHN.

112. —— my health certificate.
mi certificado de salud.
mee sayr-tee-fee-KAH-doh day sah-LOOD.

113. The bags to your left are mine.
Las maletas a su izquierda son las mías.
lahs mah-LAY-tahss ah soo eess-KYAYR-dah sohn lahs MEE-ahs.

114. I have nothing to declare.
No tengo nada que declarar.
no TEN-go NAH-dah kay day-klah-RAHR.

115. All this is for my personal use.
Todo esto es para mi uso personal.
TOH-doh ESS-toh ess PAH-rah mee OO-so payr-so-NAHL.

116. Must I open everything?
¿Tengo que abrir todo?
TEN-go kay ah-BREER TOH-doh?

117. I cannot open the trunk.
No puedo abrir el baúl.
no PWAY-doh ah-BREER el bah-OOL.

118. There is nothing here but clothing.
No hay más que ropa aquí.
no I mahss kay RROH-pah ah-KEE.

119. These are gifts.
Estos son regalos.
ESS-tohss sohn rray-GAH-lohss.

120. Are these things dutiable?
¿Hay que pagar impuestos sobre estos artículos?
I kay pah-GAHR eem-PWESS-tohss SO-bray ESS-tohss ahr-TEE-koo-lohss?

121. How much must I pay?
¿Cuánto tengo que pagar?
KWAHN-toh TEN-go kay pah-GAHR?

122. This is all I have.

Esto es todo lo que tengo.

ESS-toh ess TOH-doh lo kay TEN-go.

123. Have you finished?

¿Ha terminado usted?

ah tayr-mee-NAH-doh oos-TED?

BAGGAGE

124. Where can I check my baggage through to Buenos Aires?

¿Dónde puedo hacer enviar mi equipaje a Buenos Aires?

DOHN-day PWAY-doh ah-SER en-VYAHR mee ay-kee-PAH-hay ah BWAY-nohss I-rayss?

125. The baggage room.

La sala de equipajes.

lah SAH-lah day ay-kee-PAH-hess.

126. The baggage check.

El recibo de equipajes.

el ray-SEE-bo day ay-kee-PAH-hess.

127. I want to leave these packages for a while.

Quiero dejar estos paquetes un rato.

KYAY-ro day-HAHR ESS-tohss pah-KAY-tess oon RRAH-toh.

128. Handle this very carefully.

Mucho cuidado con esto.

MOO-cho kwee-DAH-doh kohn ESS-toh.

129. Put everything in a taxi.

Ponga todo en un taxi.

POHN-gah TOH-doh en oon TAHK-see.

TRAVEL: GENERAL EXPRESSIONS

SIDE TWO—BAND I

130. I want to go [to the airline office].
Quiero ir [a la oficina de la línea aérea].
KYAY-ro eer [ah lah o-fee-SEE-nah day lah LEE-nay-ah ah-AY-ray-ah].

131.—— to the travel agent's office.
a la oficina del agente de viajes.
ah lah o-fee-SEE-nah del ah-HEN-tay day VYAH-hays.

132. How long does it take to go to Madrid?
¿En cuánto tiempo se llega a Madrid?
en KWAHN-toh TYEM-po say YAY-gah ah mah-DREED?

133. When will we arrive at Barcelona?
¿Cuándo llegaremos a Barcelona?
KWAHN-doh yay-gah-RAY-mohss ah bahr-say-LO-nah?

134. Is this the direct way to the Prado?
¿Es éste el camino directo al Prado?
ess ESS-tay el kah-MEE-no dee-REK-toh ahl PRAH-doh?

135. Please show me the way [to the business section].
Por favor dígame cómo se llega [al centro].
por fah-VOR DEE-gah-may KO-mo say YAY-gah [ahl SEN-tro].

136.—— to the residential section.
a la sección residencial.
ah lah sek-SYOHN ray-see-den-SYAHL.

137. —— **to the city.**
a la ciudad.
ah lah syoo-DAHD.

138. —— **to the village.**
al pueblo.
ahl PWAY-blo.

139. Where do I turn?
¿Dónde doy vuelta?
DOHN-day doy VWELL-tah?

140. —— **to the north.**
al norte.
ahl NOR-tay.

141. —— **to the south.**
al sur.
ahl soor.

142. —— **to the east.**
al este.
ahl ESS-tay.

143. —— **to the west.**
al oeste.
ahl o-ESS-tay.

144. —— **to the right.**
a la derecha.
ah lah day-RAY-chah.

145. —— **to the left.**
a la izquierda.
ah lah eess-KYAYR-dah.

146. —— **at the traffic light.**
dónde está el semáforo.
DOHN-day ess-TAH el say-MAH-fo-ro.

147. Where is it?
¿Dónde está?
DOHN-day ess-TAH?

148. This way.
Por aquí.
por ah-KEE.

149. That way.
Por allí.
por ah-YEE.

150. Is it [on this side of the street]?
¿Está [de este lado de la calle]?
ess-TAH [day ESS-tay LAH-doh day lah KAH-yay]?

151. —— on the other side of the street.
del otro lado de la calle.
del O-tro LAH-doh day lah KAH-yay.

152. —— at the corner.
en la esquina.
en lah ess-KEE-nah.

153. —— in the middle.
en medio.
en MAY-dyoh.

154. —— straight ahead.
adelante.
ah-day-LAHN-tay.

155. —— inside the station.
dentro de la estación.
DEN-troh day lah ess-tah-SYOHN.

156. —— outside the lobby.
fuera del lobby.
FWAY-rah del "lobby."

157. —— opposite the park.
frente al parque.
FREN-tay ahl PAHR-kay.

158. —— behind the school.
detrás de la escuela.
day-TRAHSS day lah ess-KWAY-lah.

159. —— in front of the monument.
frente al monumento.
FREN-tay ahl mo-noo-MAYN-toh.

160. —— forward.
adelante.
ah-day-LAHN-tay.

161. —— back.
atrás.
ah-TRAHSS.

162. How far is it?
¿A qué distancia está?
ah kay deess-TAHN-syah ess-TAH?

163. Is it [near] far?
¿Está [cerca] lejos?
ess-TAH [SAYR-kah] LAY-hohss?

164. Can I walk there?
¿Puedo llegar a pie?
PWAY-doh yay-GAHR ah pyay?

165. Am I going in the right direction?
¿Voy bien?
voy byen?

166. What street is this?
¿Qué calle es ésta?
kay KAH-yay ess ESS-tah?

TICKETS

SIDE TWO—BAND 2

167. Where is the ticket office?
¿Dónde está la taquilla?
DOHN-day ess-TAH lah tah-KEE-yah?

168. How much is [a round-trip ticket] to Caracas?

¿Cuánto cuesta [un billete de ida y vuelta] a Caracas?

KWAHN-toh KWESS-tah [oon bee-YAY-tay day EE-dah ee VWELL-tah] ah kah-RAH-kahss?

169. —— a one-way ticket.

un billete sencillo.

oon bee-YAY-tay sen-SEE-yo.

170. First class.

Primera clase.

pree-MAY-rah KLAH-say.

171. Second class.

Segunda clase.

say-GOON-dah KLAH-say.

172. Third class.

Tercera clase.

tayr-SAY-rah KLAH-say.

173. Local.

Local.

lo-KAHL.

174. Express.

Rápido.

RAH-pee-doh.

175. A reserved seat.

Un asiento apartado.

oon ah-SYEN-toh ah-pahr-TAH-doh.

176. The waiting room.

La sala de espera.

lah SAH-lah day ess-PAY-rah.

177. May I stop at Seville on the way?

¿Puedo parar en Sevilla en camino?

PWAY-doh pah-RAHR en say-VEE-yah en kah-MEE-no?

178. Can I get something to eat on the way?
¿Se puede comer en camino?
say PWAY-day ko-MAYR en kah-MEE-no?

BOAT

179. When must I go on board?
¿A qué hora debo estar a bordo?
ah kay O-rah DAY-bo ess-TAHR ah BOHR-doh?

180. Bon voyage.
Buen viaje.
bwen VYAH-hay.

181. The captain.
El capitán.
el kah-pee-TAHN.

182. The purser.
El contador.
el kohn-tah-DOR.

183. The steward.
El camarero.
el kah-mah-RAY-ro.

184. The cabin.
El camarote.
el kah-mah-RO-tay.

185. The deck.
La cubierta.
lah koo-BYAYR-tah.

186. The deck chair.
La silla de cubierta.
lah SEE-yah day koo-BYAYR-tah.

187. The lifeboat.
La lancha.
lah LAHN-chah.

188. The dock.
El muelle.
el MWAY-yay.

189. The life preserver.
El salvavidas.
el sahl-vah-VEE-dahss.

190. Dramamine.
Dramamina.
drah-mah-MEE-nah.

191. I feel seasick.
Estoy mareado.
ess-TOY mah-ray-AH-doh.

AIRPLANE

192. Is there bus service to the airport?
¿Hay servicio de transporte al aeropuerto?
*I sayr-VEE-syoh day trahnss-POR-tay ahl ah-ay-ro-
PWAYR-toh?*

193. At what time will they come for me?
¿A qué hora vienen por mí?
ah kay O-rah VYAY-nen por mee?

194. Is flight 23 on time?
¿Está a tiempo el vuelo veintitrés?
*ess-TAH ah TYEM-po el VWAY-lo vayn-tee-
TRAYSS?*

195. How many kilos may I take?
¿Cuántos kilos puedo llevar?
KWAHN-tohss KEE-lohss PWAY-doh yay-VAHR?

196. How much per kilo for excess?
¿Cuánto por kilo de exceso?
KWAHN-toh por KEE-lo day ek-SAY-so?

TRAIN

SIDE TWO—BAND 3

197. Where is the railroad station?
¿Dónde está la estación de ferrocarriles?
DOHN-day ess-TAH lah ess-tah-SYOHN day fay-rro-kah-RREE-less?

198. When does the train for Oaxaca leave?
¿Cuándo sale el tren para Oaxaca?
KWAHN-doh SAH-lay el tren PAH-rah wah-HAH-kah?

199. The arrival.
La llegada.
lah yay-GAH-dah.

200. The departure.
La salida.
lah sah-LEE-dah.

201. From what track does the train leave?
¿De cuál andén sale el tren?
day kwahl ahn-DAYN SAH-lay el trayn?

202. Please [open the window].
Favor de [abrir la ventanilla].
fah-VOR day [ah-BREER lah ven-tah-NEE-yah].

203. —— close the window.
cerrar la ventanilla.
say-RRAHR lah ven-tah-NEE-yah.

204. Where is [the diner].
¿Dónde está [el comedor]?
DOHN-day ess-TAH [el ko-may-DOR]?

205. ——the sleeper.
el coche-cama.
el KOH-chay-KAH-mah.

206. Where is the smoking car?
¿Dónde queda el coche fumador?
DOHN-day KAY-dah el KOH-chay foo-mah-DOHR?

207. May I smoke?
¿Se puede fumar?
say PWAY-day foo-MAHR?

BUS AND STREETCAR

208. What streetcar do I take to the plaza?
¿Qué tranvía tomo para la plaza?
kay trahn-VEE-ah TOH-mo PAH-rah lah PLAH-sah?

209. The bus stop.
La parada.
lah pah-RAH-dah.

210. A transfer.
Un transbordo.
oon trahnss-BOR-doh.

211. Where does the streetcar for the main street stop?
¿Dónde para el tranvía que va a la calle principal?
DOHN-day PAH-rah el trahn-VEE-ah kay vah ah lah KAH-yay preen-see-PAHL?

212. Does the bus stop at the avenue?
¿Para este autobús en la avenida?
PAH-rah ESS-tay ow-toh-BOOSS en lah ah-vay-NEE-dah?

213. Do you go near the circle?
¿Pasa usted por la rotonda?
PAH-sah oos-TED por lah ro-TOHN-dah?

214. Do I have to change?
¿Tengo que cambiar?
TEN-go kay kahm-BYAHR?

215. Driver, please tell me where to get off.
Conductor, por favor, avíseme dónde me bajo.
kohn-dook-TOHR, por fah-VOR, ah-VEE-say-may DOHN-day may BAH-ho.

216. I want to get off at the next stop.
Quiero bajarme en la próxima parada.
KYAY-ro bah-HAHR-may en lah PROHK-see-mah pah-RAH-dah.

TAXI

217. Please call a taxi for me.
Haga el favor de llamarme un taxi.
AH-gah el fah-VOR day yah-MAHR-may oon TAHK-see.

218. Are you free?
¿Está libre?
ess-TAH LEE-bray?

219. What do you charge [per hour]?
¿Cuánto cobra [por hora]?
KWAHN-toh KO-brah [por O-rah]?

220. —— per kilometer.
por kilómetro.
por kee-LO-may-troh.

221. Please drive [more slowly].
Por favor, conduzca [más despacio].
por fah-VOR, kohn-DOOSS-kah [mahss dess-PAH-syoh].

222. —— more carefully.
con más cuidado.
kohn mahss kwee-DAH-doh.

223. Stop here.
Pare aquí.
PAH-ray ah-KEE.

224. Wait for me.
Espéreme.
ess-PAY-ray-may.

AUTOMOBILE TRAVEL*

SIDE TWO—BAND 4

225. Where can I rent a car?
¿Dónde puedo alquilar un auto?
DOHN-day PWAY-doh ahl-kee-LAHR oon OW-toh?

226. I have an international driver's license.
Tengo una licencia internacional.
TEN-go OO-nah lee-SEN-syah een-tayr-nah-syoh-NAHL.

227. A gas station.
Un expendio de gasolina.
oon es-PEN-dyoh day gah-so-LEE-nah.

228. A garage.
Un garaje.
oon gah-RAH-hay.

229. A mechanic.
Un mecánico.
oon may-KAH-nee-ko.

230. Is the road [good] bad?
¿Está el camino en [buenas] malas condiciones?
ess-TAH el kah-MEE-no en [BWAY-nahss] MAH-lahss kohn-dee-SYOH-ness?

* An extensive unrecorded listing of Road Signs appears on page 112.

231. Where does that road go?
¿Adónde conduce aquel camino?
ah-DOHN-day kohn-DOO-say ah-KEL kah-MEE-no?

232. What town is this?
¿Cómo se llama este pueblo?
KO-mo say YAH-mah ESS-tay PWAY-blo?

233. The next one?
¿El próximo?
el PROHK-see-mo?

234. Can you show me on the map?
¿Puede indicarme en el mapa?
PWAY-day een-dee-KAHR-may en el MAH-pah?

235. How much is gas a liter?
¿Cuánto cuesta la gasolina por litro?
KWAHN-toh KWESS-tah lah gah-so-LEE-nah por LEE-troh?

236. The tank is [empty] full.
El tanque está [vacío] lleno.
el TAHN-kay ess-TAH [vah-SEE-o] YAY-no.

237. Give me forty liters.
Déme cuarenta litros.
DAY-may kwah-REN-tah LEE-trohss.

238. Please change the oil.
Por favor, cambie el aceite.
por fah-VOR, KAHM-byay el ah-SAY-tay.

239. Put water in the battery.
Ponga agua en el acumulador.
POHN-gah AH-gwah en el ah-koo-moo-lah-DOR.

240. Will you lubricate the car?
¿Quiere engrasar el coche?
KYAY-ray en-grah-SAHR el KO-chay?

241. Clean the windshield.
Límpieme el parabrisas.
LEEM-pyay-may el pah-rah-BREE-sahss.

242. Adjust the brakes.
Ajuste los frenos.
ah-HOOSS-tay lohss FRAY-nohss.

243. Will you check the tires?
¿Quiere usted revisar las llantas?
KYAY-ray oos-TED rray-vee-SAHR lahss YAHN-tahss?

244. Can you fix [the flat tire] now?
¿Puede componerme [la llanta] ahora?
PWAY-day kohm-po-NAYR-may [lah YAHN-tah] ah-O-rah?

245. —— a puncture.
un pinchazo.
oon peen-CHAH-so.

246. —— a slow leak.
un escape.
oon ess-KAH-pay.

247. The engine overheats.
El motor se calienta.
el mo-TOHR say kah-LYEN-tah.

248. The motor [misses] stalls.
El motor [falla] se para.
el mo-TOHR [FAH-yah] say PAH-rah.

249. May I park here for a while?
¿Me permite estacionarme aquí un rato?
may payr-MEE-tay ess-tah-syoh-NAHR-may ah-KEE oon RRAH-toh?

PARTS OF THE CAR

250. The accelerator.
El acelerador.
el ah-say-lay-rah-DOHR.

251. The battery.
El acumulador.
el ah-koo-moo-lah-DOHR.

252. The clutch.
El embrague.
el em-BRAH-gay.

253. The gear shift.
La palanca de velocidades.
lah pah-LAHN-kah day vay-lo-see-DAH-dayss.

254. The headlight.
El fanal.
el fah-NAHL.

255. The horn.
La bocina.
lah bo-SEE-nah.

256. The spare tire.
La llanta de repuesto.
lah YAHN-tah day rray-PWESS-toh.

257. The spring.
El muelle.
el MWAY-yay.

258. The starter.
El arranque.
el ah-RRAHN-kay.

259. The steering wheel.
El volante.
el vo-LAHN-tay.

260. The wheel.
La rueda.
lah RRWAY-dah.

AT THE HOTEL

SIDE THREE—BAND I

261. I am looking for [a good hotel].
Busco [un buen hotel].
BOOS-ko [oon bwayn o-TEL].

262. —— the best hotel.
el mejor hotel.
el may-HOHR o-TEL.

263. —— an inexpensive hotel.
un hotel barato.
oon o-TEL bah-RAH-toh.

264. —— a boarding house.
una casa de huéspedes.
OO-nah KAH-sah day WESS-pay-dayss.

265. —— a furnished apartment.
un apartamiento amueblado.
*oon ah-pahr-tah-MYEN-toh ah-mway-BLAH-
doh.*

266. I (do not) want to be in the center of town.
(No) quiero estar en el centro.
(no) KYAY-ro ess-TAHR en el SEN-tro.

267. Where it is not noisy.
Dónde no haya ruido.
DOHN-day no AH-yah RRWEE-doh.

268. I have a reservation for today.
Tengo reservado para hoy.
TEN-go rray-sayr-VAH-doh PAH-rah oy.

269. Do you have [a vacancy]?
¿Tiene [cuarto]?
TYAY-nay [KWAHR-toh]?

270. —— an air-conditioned room.
un cuarto con aire acondicionado.
oon KWAHR-toh kohn I-ray ah-kohn-dee-syoh-NAH-doh.

271. —— a single room.
un cuarto para uno.
oon KWAHR-toh PAH-rah OO-no.

272. —— a double room.
un cuarto para dos.
oon KWAHR-toh PAH-rah dohss.

273. I want a room [for tonight].
Quiero un cuarto [para esta noche].
KYAY-ro oon KWAHR-toh [PAH-rah ESS-tah No-chay].

274. —— for two persons.
para dos personas.
PAH-rah dohss payr-SOH-nahss.

275. —— with a double bed.
con cama matrimonial.
kohn KAH-mah mah-tree-mo-NYAHL.

276. —— with twin beds.
con camas gemelas.
kohn KAH-mahss hay-MAY-lahss.

277. —— with a bath.
con baño.
kohn BAH-nyoh.

278. —— with a shower.
con ducha.
kohn DOO-chah.

279. —— with a sink.
con lavabo.
kohn lah-VAH-bo.

280. —— **with a balcony.**
con balcón.
kohn bahl-KOHN.

281. —— **without meals.**
sin comidas.
seen koh-MEE-dahs.

282. **What is the rate per day?**
¿Cuánto cuesta por día?
KWAHN-toh KWESS-tah por DEE-ah?

283. **I should like to see the room.**
Quisiera ver el cuarto.
kee-SYAY-rah vayr el KWAHR-toh.

284. **Is it [upstairs] downstairs?**
¿Está [arriba] abajo?
ess-TAH [ah-RREE-bah] ah-BAH-ho?

285. **Is there an elevator?**
¿Hay ascensor?
I ah-sen-SOR?

286. **Room service, please.**
Servicio de cuarto, por favor.
sayr-VEE-syoh day KWAHR-toh, por fah-VOR.

287. **Please send [a porter] to my room.**
Haga el favor de mandar [un mozo] a mi cuarto.
*AH-gah el fah-VOR day mahn-DAHR [oon MO-so]
ah mee KWAHR-toh.*

288. —— **a chambermaid.**
una camarera.
OO-nah kah-mah-RAY-rah.

289. —— **a bellhop.**
un botones.
oon bo-TOH-ness.

290. Please call me at nine A.M.
Haga el favor de llamarme a las nueve de la
mañana.
*AH-gah el fah-VOR day yah-MAHR-may ah lahss
NWAY-vay day lah mah-NYAH-nah.*

291. I want breakfast in my room.
Quiero el desayuno en mi cuarto.
KYAY-ro el dess-ah-YOO-no en mee KWAHR-toh.

292. Who is it?
¿Quién es?
kyen ess?

293. Come back later.
Vuelva más tarde.
VWAYL-vah mahss TAHR-day.

294. Bring me [a blanket].
Tráigame [una frazada].
TRY-gah-may [OO-nah frah-SAH-dah].

295. —— a pillow.
una almohada.
OO-nah ahl-mo-AH-dah.

296. —— a pillowcase.
una funda.
OO-nah FOON-dah.

297. —— some hangers.
ganchos.
GAHN-chohss.

298. —— some soap.
jabón.
hah-BOHN.

299. —— some towels.
toallas.
toh-AH-yahss.

300. —— a bath mat.
un tapete de baño.
oon tah-PAY-tay day BAH-nyoh.

301. —— some toilet paper.
papel higiénico.
pah-PEL ee-HYAY-nee-ko.

302. I should like to speak to the manager.
Quisiera hablar con el gerente.
kee-SYAY-rah ah-BLAHR kohn el hay-REN-tay.

303. My room key, please.
Mi llave, por favor.
mee YAH-vay, por fah-VOR.

304. Have I any letters or messages?
¿Hay cartas o mensajes para mí?
I KAHR-tahss o men-SAH-hess PAH-rah mee?

305. What is my room number?
¿Cuál es el número de mi cuarto?
kwahl ess el NOO-may-ro day mee KWAHR-toh?

306. I am leaving at ten o'clock.
Salgo a las diez.
SAHL-go ah lahss dyayss.

307. Please make out my bill as soon as possible.
Favor de preparar mi cuenta lo más pronto
posible.
*fah-VOR day pray-pah-RAHR mee KWEN-tah lo
mahss PROHN-toh po-SEE-blay.*

308. Is everything included?
¿Está todo incluído?
ess-TAH TOH-doh een-kloo-EE-doh?

**309. Please forward my mail to American
Express in Valparaíso.**
Favor de reexpedirme las cartas al American
Express en Valparaíso.
*fah-VOR day rray-ex-pay-DEER-may lahss KAHR-
tahss ahl American Express en vahl-pah-rah-EE-so*

AT THE CAFÉ

SIDE THREE—BAND 2

310. Bartender, I'd like to have [a drink].
  Cantinero, quisiera [una bebida].
  kahn-tee-NAY-ro, kee-SYAY-rah [OO-nah bay-BEE-dah].

311. —— a cocktail.
  un cocktail.
  oon "cocktail."

312. —— a bottle of mineral water.
  una botella de agua mineral.
  OO-nah bo-TAY-yah day AH-gwah mee-nay-RAHL.

313. —— a glass of sherry.
  un vaso de jerez.
  oon VAH-so day hay-RAYSS.

314. —— some whiskey (and soda).
  whiskey (y soda).
  WEES-kee (ee SO-dah).

315. —— some cognac.
  coñac.
  ko-NYAHK.

316. —— some champagne.
  champaña.
  chahm-PAH-nyah.

317. —— a liqueur.
  un licor.
  oon lee-KOHR.

318. —— some light (dark) beer.
  cerveza clara (oscura).
  sayr-VAY-sah KLAH-rah (ohss-KOO-rah).

319. —— **some red (white) wine.**
         vino tinto (blanco).
         VEE-no TEEN-toh (BLAHN-ko).

320. **Let's have another.**
     Tomemos otro más.
     toh-MAY-mohss O-tro mahss.

321. **To your health!**
     Salud!
     sah-LOOD!

AT THE RESTAURANT
SIDE THREE—BAND 3

322. **Can you recommend a native restaurant [for dinner]?**
     ¿Puede recomendar un restaurante típico [para la comida]?
     PWAY-day rray-koh-men-DAHR oon res-tow-RAHN-tay TEE-pee-ko [PAH-rah lah ko-MEE-dah]?

323. —— **for breakfast.**
         para el desayuno.
         PAH-rah el dess-ah-YOO-no.

324. —— **for lunch.**
         para el almuerzo.
         PAH-rah el ahl-MWAYR-so.

325. —— **for a sandwich.**
         para un sandwich.
         PAH-rah oon "sandwich."

326. **At what time is supper served?**
     ¿A qué hora se sirve la cena?
     ah kay OH-rah say SEER-vay lah SAY-nah?

327. **The waitress.**
     La camarera.
     lah kah-mah-RAY-rah.

328. The waiter.
El camarero.
el kah-mah-RAY-ro.

329. The headwaiter.
El jefe de camareros.
el HAY-fay day kah-mah-RAY-rohss.

330. Give me a table for two near the window.
Déme una mesa para dos cerca de la ventana.
DAY-may OO-nah MAY-sah PAH-rah dohss SAYR-kah day lah ven-TAH-nah.

331. We want to dine [à la carte] table d'hôte.
Deseamos comer [a la carta] comida corrida.
day-say-AH-mohss ko-MAYR [ah lah KAHR-tah] ko-MEE-dah ko-RREE-dah.

332. Please serve us quickly.
Haga el favor de servirnos de prisa.
AH-gah el fah-VOR day sayr-VEER-nohss day PREE-sah.

333. Bring me [the menu].
Tráigame [la carta].
TRY-gah-may [lah KAHR-tah].

334. —— the wine list.
la carta de vinos.
lah KAHR-tah day VEE-nohss.

335. —— a napkin.
una servilleta.
OO-nah sayr-vee-YAY-tah.

336. —— a fork.
un tenedor.
oon tay-nay-DOHR.

337. —— a knife.
un cuchillo.
oon koo-CHEE-yoh.

338. —— **a plate.**
un plato.
oon PLAH-toh.

339. —— **a teaspoon.**
una cucharita.
OO-nah koo-chah-REE-tah.

340. —— **a large spoon.**
una cuchara.
OO-nah koo-CHAH-rah.

341. I want [simple] food.
Quiero comida [sencilla].
KYAY-ro ko-MEE-dah sen-SEE-yah.

342. —— **not too fat.**
no muy grasosa.
no mwee grah-SO-sah.

343. —— **not too sweet.**
no muy dulce.
no mwee DOOL-say.

344. —— **not too spicy.**
no muy condimentada.
no mwee kohn-dee-men-TAH-dah.

345. —— **cooked.**
cocida.
ko-SEE-dah.

346. —— **fried.**
frita.
FREE-tah.

347. —— **boiled.**
hervida.
ayr-VEE-dah.

348. I like the meat [rare].
Me gusta la carne [cruda].
may GOOSS-tah lah KAHR-nay [KROO-dah].

349. —— medium.
mediana.
may-DYAH-nah.

350. —— well done.
bien cocida.
byen ko-SEE-dah.

351. A little more.
Un poco más.
oon PO-ko mahss.

352. Enough.
Suficiente.
soo-fee-SYEN-tay.

353. This is not clean.
Esto no está limpio.
ESS-toh no ess-TAH LEEM-pyoh.

354. This is cold.
Esto está frío.
ESS-toh ess-TAH FREE-o.

355. I did not order this.
No he pedido esto.
no ay pay-DEE-doh ESS-toh.

356. Take it away, please.
Lléveselo, por favor.
YAY-vay-say-lo, por fah-VOR.

357. May I change this for a salad?
¿Se puede cambiar esto por una ensalada?
*say PWAY-day kahm-BYAHR ESS-toh por OO-nah
en-sah-LAH-dah?*

358. The check, please.
La cuenta, por favor.
lah KWEN-tah, por fah-VOR.

359. Are the tip and service charge included?
¿Están incluídos la propina y el servicio?
ess-TAHN een-kloo-EE-dohss lah pro-PEE-nah ee el sayr-VEE-syoh?

360. There is a mistake in the bill.
Hay un error en la cuenta.
I oon ay-RROR en lah KWEN-tah.

361. What are these charges for?
¿Qué son estos extras?
kay sohn ESS-tohss EKS-trahss?

362. Keep the change.
Quédese con el cambio.
KAY-day-say kohn el KAHM-byoh.

363. The food and service are excellent.
La comida y el servicio son excelentes.
lah ko-MEE-dah ee el sayr-VEE-syoh sohn ek-say-LEN-tays.

364. Hearty appetite!
¡Buen apetito!
bwayn ah-pay-TEE-toh!

FOOD LIST

365. Drinking water.
Agua para beber.
AH-gwah PAH-rah bay-BAYR.

366. —— with ice.
con hielo.
kohn YAY-lo.

367. —— without ice.
sin hielo.
seen YAY-lo.

368. The bread.
El pan.
el pahn.

369. The butter.
La mantequilla.
lah mahn-tay-KEE-yah.

370. The sugar.
El azúcar.
el ah-SOO-kahr.

371. The salt.
La sal.
lah sahl.

372. The pepper.
La pimienta.
lah pee-MYEN-tah.

373. The oil.
El aceite.
el ah-SAY-tay.

374. The vinegar.
El vinagre.
el vee-NAH-gray.

375. The garlic.
El ajo.
el AH-ho.

376. The catsup.
La salsa de tomate.
lah SAHL-sah day toh-MAH-tay.

377. The mustard.
La mostaza.
lah mohss-TAH-sah.

378. The sauce.
La salsa.
lah SAHL-sah.

BREAKFAST FOODS

SIDE FOUR—BAND I

379. I would like [fruit juice].
Me gustaría [jugo de fruta].
may goos-tah-REE-ah [HOO-go day FROO-tah].

380. —— orange juice.
jugo de naranja.
HOO-go day nah-RAHN-hah.

381. —— tomato juice.
jugo de tomate.
HOO-go day toh-MAH-tay.

382. —— stewed prunes.
ciruelas pasas.
see-RWAY-lahs PAH-sas.

383. —— cooked cereal.
cereal cocido.
say-ree-AHL ko-SEE-doh.

384. —— toast and jam.
tostada con conserva.
tohss-TAH-dah kohn kohn-SAYR-vah.

385. —— rolls.
panecillos.
pah-nay-SEE-yohss.

386. —— an omelette.
una tortilla.
OO-nah tohr-TEE-yah.

387. —— soft-boiled eggs.
huevos tibios.
WAY-vohss TEE-byohss.

388. —— four-minute eggs.
huevos pasados por agua— cuatro minutos.
WAY-vohss pah-SAH-dohss por AH-gwah
    KWAH-tro mee-NOO-tohss.

389. —— hard-boiled eggs.
   huevos duros.
   WAY-vohss DOO-rohss.
390. —— fried eggs.
   huevos fritos.
   WAY-vohss FREE-tohss.
391. —— scrambled eggs.
   huevos revueltos.
   WAY-vohss rray-VWEL-tohss.
392. —— eggs with bacon.
   huevos con tocino.
   WAY-vohss kohn toh-SEE-no.
393. —— eggs with ham.
   huevos con jamón.
   WAY-vohss kohn hah-MOHN.

SOUPS AND ENTRÉES

394. I would like [chicken soup].
   Quisiera [sopa de pollo].
   kee-see-AY-rah [SO-pah day PO-yo].
395. —— vegetable soup.
   sopa de legumbres.
   SO-pah day lay-GOOM-brayss.
396. —— anchovies.
   anchoas.
   ahn-CHO-ahss.
397. —— beef.
   carne de vaca.
   KAHR-nay day VAH-kah.
398. —— roast beef.
   rosbif.
   rrohss-BEEF.

399. —— broiled chicken.
pollo a la parrilla.
PO-yo ah lah pah-RREE-yah.

400. —— fried chicken.
pollo frito.
PO-yo FREE-toh.

401. —— duck.
pato.
PAH-toh.

402. —— fish.
pescado.
pess-KAH-doh.

403. —— goose.
ganso.
GAHN-so.

404. —— lamb.
cordero.
kor-DAY-ro.

405. —— liver.
hígado.
EE-gah-doh.

406. —— lobster.
langosta.
lahn-GOHSS-tah.

407. —— oysters.
ostras.
OSS-trahss.

408. —— pork.
puerco.
PWAYR-ko.

409. —— sardines.
sardinas.
sahr-DEE-nahss.

410. —— sausage.
salchicha.
sahl-CHEE-chah.

411. —— shrimp.
camarones.
kah-mah-RO-ness.

412. —— steak.
bisté.
beess-TAY.

413. —— veal.
ternera.
tayr-NAY-rah.

VEGETABLES AND SALAD

414. I want some [asparagus].
Quiero [espárragos].
KYAY-ro [ess-PAH-rrah-gohss].

415. —— beans.
frijoles.
free-HO-less.

416. —— cabbage.
col.
kohl.

417. —— carrots.
zanahorias.
sah-nah-OHR-yahss.

418. —— cauliflower.
coliflor.
ko-lee-FLOHR.

419. —— celery and olives.
apio y aceitunas.
AH-pyoh ee ah-say-TOO-nahss.

420. —— **cucumber.**
pepino.
pay-PEE-noh.

421. —— **lettuce.**
lechuga.
lay-CHOO-gah.

422. —— **mushrooms.**
hongos.
OHN-gohss.

423. —— **onions.**
cebollas.
say-BO-yahss.

424. —— **peas.**
guisantes.
ghee-SAHN-tess.

425. —— **peppers.**
pimientos.
pee-MYEN-tohss.

426. —— **pimentos.**
pimentón.
pee-men-TOHN.

427. —— **boiled potatoes.**
patatas hervidas.
pah-TAH-tahss ayr-VEE-dahss.

428. —— **mashed potatoes.**
puré de papas.
poo-RAY day PAH-pahss.

429. —— **baked potatoes.**
patatas al horno.
pah-TAH-tahss ahl OR-no.

430. —— **fried potatoes.**
patatas fritas.
pah-TAH-tahss FREE-tahss.

431. —— **rice.**
arroz.
ah-RROHSS.

432. —— **spinach.**
espinacas.
ess-pee-NAH-kahss.

433. —— **tomatoes.**
tomates.
toh-MAH-tays.

FRUITS

434. Do you have [an apple]?
¿Tiene [una manzana]?
TYAY-nay [OO-nah mahn-SAH-nah]?

435. —— **cherries.**
cerezas.
say-RAY-sahss.

436. —— **a grapefruit.**
una toronja.
OO-nah toh-ROHN-hah.

437. —— **grapes.**
uvas.
OO-vahss.

438. —— **lemon.**
limón.
lee-MOHN.

439. —— **melon.**
melón.
may-LOHN.

440. —— **an orange.**
una naranja.
OO-nah nah-RAHN-hah.

441. —— **a peach.**
     un melocotón.
     oon may-lo-ko-TOHN.
442. —— **raspberries.**
     frambuesas.
     frahm-BWAY-sahss.
443. —— **strawberries.**
     fresas.
     FRAY-sahss.

BEVERAGES

444. **A cup of black coffee.**
     Una taza de café solo.
     OO-nah TAH-sah day kah-FAY SO-lo.
445. **Coffee with cream.**
     Café con crema.
     kah-FAY kohn KRAY-mah.
446. **A glass of milk.**
     Un vaso de leche.
     oon VAH-so day LAY-chay.
447. **Tea.**
     Té.
     tay.
448. **Lemonade.**
     Limonada.
     lee-mo-NAH-dah.

DESSERTS

449. **We would like [some cake].**
     Quisiéramos [torta].
     kee-SYAY-rah-mohss [TOHR-tah].

450. —— **a piece of pie.**
   pastel.
   pahs-TEL.

451. —— **some cheese.**
   queso.
   KAY-so.

452. —— **some cookies.**
   galletas.
   gah-YAY-tahss.

453. —— **some custard.**
   flan.
   flahn.

454. —— **some chocolate ice cream.**
   helado de chocolate.
   ay-LAH-doh day cho-ko-LAH-tay.

455. —— **some vanilla ice cream.**
   helado de vainilla.
   ay-LAH-doh day vie-NEE-yah.

AT THE RESTAURANT

(Conversation at normal rate of speech)

456. ¿Van a tomar algo antes de comer?
   Would you like to have something before your dinner?

457. Sí. Un vermouth cassis, un jerez y una botella de vino blanco.
   Yes. One vermouth cassis, one glass of sherry, and a bottle of white wine.

458. ¿Quieren pedir la comida ahora mismo?
   Do you want to order right now?

459. ¿Qué nos recomienda usted? ¿Cuál es la
especialidad de la casa?

What do you recommend? What is the specialty
of the house?

460. El bisté está muy bueno hoy. El filete de
sol también está muy sabroso.

The beef tenderloin is especially good today. The
filet of sole is also very tasty.

461. Un bisté y una langosta.

One beef tenderloin and one lobster.

462. Háganme el favor de elegir dos legumbres.

Please choose two vegetables.

463. Patatas al horno y guisantes con el bisté;
cebollas al gratin y espárragos con salsa
de mantequilla con la langosta.

Baked potatoes and peas with the beef; onions
au gratin and asparagus with butter sauce with
the lobster.

464. ¿Y para comenzar?

And to begin with?

465. Arenque en escabeche y un coctel de fruta.
Sopa de guisantes y sopa de pollo.

Marinated herring and one fruit cup. Pea soup
and chicken soup.

466. ¿Ensalada?

Salad?

467. Sí, una ensalada de lechuga con tomates,
aceite y vinagre. No le ponga ajo.

Yes, a lettuce and tomato salad, oil and vinegar.
No garlic.

468. ¿Desean tomar café con la comida?
Would you like coffee with your dinner?

469. No. El café lo tomaremos más tarde, con el postre.
No. We'll have coffee later, with the dessert.

470. Muchas gracias.
Thanks.

471. Para postre tenemos: helado de chocolate, vainilla y fresa; pasteles surtidos; queso Camembert y suizo; tartaletas de frambuesa.
For dessert we have: chocolate, vanilla, and strawberry ice cream; assorted pastries; Camembert and Swiss cheese; raspberry tarts.

472. Un helado de chocolate. Una tartaleta de frambuesa. Un café solo. Té con leche. Y camarero, hágame el favor de traerme otra cuchara. Esta no está limpia.
One chocolate ice cream. One raspberry tart. A cup of black coffee. Tea with milk. And waiter, please bring me another spoon. This one isn't clean.

473. Lo siento.
I'm so sorry.

474. La cuenta, por favor. No tenemos mucho tiempo porque vamos al teatro.
The check, please. We don't have much time because we are going to the theatre.

475. Muy bien, señor.
Very well, sir.

CHURCH

SIDE FOUR—BAND 2

476. Is there an English-speaking [priest]?
¿Hay algún [cura] que hable inglés?
I ahl-GOON [KOO-rah] kay AH-blay een-GLAYSS?

477. A rabbi.
Un rabino.
oon rah-BEE-no.

478. A minister.
Un ministro.
oon mee-NEESS-tro.

479. A [Catholic] Protestant church.
Una iglesia [católica] protestante.
OO-nah ee-GLAY-syah [kah-TOH-lee-kah] pro-tess-TAHN-tay.

480. A synagogue.
Una sinagoga.
OO-nah see-nah-GO-gah.

481. When is [the service] the mass?
¿A qué hora es [el servicio] la misa?
ah kay O-rah ess [el sayr-VEE-syoh] lah MEE-sah?

SIGHTSEEING

482. I want a licensed guide who speaks English.
Deseo un guía autorizado que hable inglés.
day-SAY-o oon GHEE-ah ow-toh-ree-SAH-doh kay AH-blay een-GLAYSS.

483. What is the charge [per hour] per day?
¿Cuánto cobra usted [por hora] por día?
KWAHN-toh KO-brah oos-TED [por O-rah] por DEE-ah?

484. I am interested in [architecture].
Me interesa [la arquitectura].
may een-tay-RAY-sah [lah ahr-kee-tek-TOO-rah].

485. —— painting.
la pintura.
lah peen-TOO-rah.

486. —— sculpture.
la escultura.
lah ess-kool-TOO-rah.

487. Show us [the castle].
Muéstrenos [el castillo].
MWESS-tray-nohss [el kahss-TEE-yoh].

488. —— the cathedral.
la catedral.
lah kah-tay-DRAHL.

489. —— the museums.
los museos.
lohss moo-SAY-ohss.

490. When does it [open] close?
¿Cuándo se [abre] cierra?
KWAHN-doh say [AH-bray] SYAY-rah?

491. Where is [the entrance]?
¿Dónde está [la entrada]?
DOHN-day ess-TAH [lah en-TRAH-dah]?

492. —— the exit.
la salida.
lah sah-LEE-dah.

AMUSEMENTS

SIDE FOUR—BAND 3

493. I should like to go [to a concert].
Quisiera ir [a un concierto].
kee-SYAY-rah eer [ah oon kohn-SYAYR-toh].

494. —— **to a matinée.**
a una matinée.
ah OO-nah mah-tee-NAY.

495. —— **to the movies.**
al cine.
ahl SEE-nay.

496. —— **to a night club.**
a un cabaret.
ah oon kah-bah-RAY.

497. —— **to the opera.**
a la ópera.
ah lah O-pay-rah.

498. —— **to the theater.**
al teatro.
ahl tay-AH-tro.

499. —— **to the box office.**
a la taquilla.
ah lah tah-KEE-yah.

500. What is playing tonight?
¿Qué dan esta noche?
kay dahn ESS-tah NO-chay?

501. When does [the evening performance] the floor show start?
¿A qué hora comienza [la función de la noche] la revista?
ah kay O-rah ko-MYEN-sah [lah foon-SYOHN day lah NO-chay] lah rray-VEESS-tah?

502. Have you [any seats] for tonight?
¿Hay [localidades] para esta noche?
I [loh-kah-lee-DAH-dayss] PAH-rah ESS-tah NO-chay?

503. —— **an orchestra seat.**
una luneta.
OO-nah loo-NAY-tah.

504. —— **a box.**
  un palco.
  oon PAHL-ko.

505. Can I see well from there?
  ¿Puedo ver bien desde allí?
  PWAY-doh vayr byen DEZ-day ah-YEE?

506. Where can we go to dance?
  ¿Adónde podemos ir a bailar?
  ah-DOHN-day po-DAY-mohss eer ah by-LAHR?

507. What is [the cover charge]?
  ¿Qué es [el precio de admisión]?
  kay ess [el PRAY-syoh day ahd-mee-SYOHN]?

508. —— **the minimum charge.**
  el mínimo.
  el MEE-nee-mo.

509. May I have this dance?
  ¿Me permite esta pieza?
  may payr-MEE-tay ESS-tah PYAY-sah?

SPORTS

510. Let's go [to the beach].
  Vamos [a la playa].
  VAH-mohss [ah la PLAH-yah].

511. —— **to the bull fights.**
  a los toros.
  ah lohss TOH-rohss.

512. —— **to the horse races.**
  a las carreras.
  ah lahss kah-RRAY-rahss.

513. —— **to the jai alai.**
  al jai-alai.
  ahl hie-ah-LIE.

514. —— **to the swimming pool.**
a la piscina.
ah lah pee-SEE-nah.

515. **I'd like to play [golf] tennis.**
Me gustaría jugar [golf] tennis.
may gooss-tah-REE-ah hoo-GAHR [golf] TAY-neess.

516. **Can we go [fishing]?**
¿Podemos ir a [pescar]?
po-DAY-mohss eer ah [pess-KAHR]?

517. —— **horseback riding.**
montar a caballo.
mohn-TAHR ah kah-BAH-yoh.

518. —— **skating.**
patinar.
pah-tee-NAHR.

519. —— **swimming.**
nadar.
nah-DAHR.

BANK AND MONEY

SIDE FIVE—BAND I

520. **Where is the nearest bank?**
¿Dónde está el banco más cercano?
DOHN-day ess-TAH el BAHN-ko mahss sayr-KAH-no?

521. **At which window can I cash this?**
¿En qué ventanilla puedo cobrar esto?
en kay ven-tah-NEE-yah PWAY-doh ko-BRAHR ESS-toh?

522. Will you cash [a personal check]?
   ¿Quiere usted cobrarme [un cheque personal]?
   KYAY-ray ooss-TED ko-BRAHR-may [oon CHAY-kay payr-so-NAHL]?

523. —— a traveler's check.
   un cheque de viajero.
   oon CHAY-kay day vyah-HAY-ro.

524. What is the exchange rate on the dollar?
   ¿A cómo está el cambio del dólar?
   ah KO-mo ess-TAH el KAHM-byoh del DOH-lahr?

525. Can you change this for me?
   ¿Puede usted cambiarme esto?
   PWAY-day ooss-TED kahm-BYAHR-may ESS-toh?

526. I want [the equivalent of fifty dollars].
   Quisiera [el equivalente de cincuenta dólares].
   kee-SYAY-rah [el ay-kee-vah-LEN-tay day seen-KWEN-tah DOH-lah-ress].

527. —— small change.
   cambio.
   KAHM-byoh.

SHOPPING

SIDE FIVE—BAND 2

528. I want to go shopping.
   Deseo ir de compras.
   day-SAY-o eer day KOHM-prahss.

529. I like this one.
   Me gusta éste.
   may GOOSS-tah ESS-tay.

530. How much is it?
   ¿Cuánto es?
   KWAHN-toh ess?

531. I prefer something [better].
Prefiero algo [mejor].
pray-FYAY-ro AHL-go [may-HOR].

532. —— cheaper.
más barato.
mahss bah-RAH-toh.

533. —— larger.
más grande.
mahss GRAHN-day.

534. —— smaller.
más pequeño.
mahss pay-KAY-nyoh.

535. Show me some others at a moderate price.
Muéstreme otros de precio módico.
MWESS-tray-may O-trohss day PRAY-syoh MO-dee-ko.

536. Is this your best price?
¿No me puede hacer una rebaja?
no may PWAY-day ah-SAYR OO-nah ray-BAH-hah?

537. May I try this on?
¿Me permite probarme esto?
may payr-MEE-tay pro-BAHR-may ESS-toh?

538. Can I order size 38?
¿Puedo mandar hacer de talla treinta y ocho?
PWAY-doh mahn-DAHR ah-SAYR day TAH-yah TRAYN-tah ee O-cho?

539. Please take [the measurements].
Haga el favor de tomarme [las medidas].
AH-gah el fah-VOR day toh-MAHR-may [lahss may-DEE-dahss].

540. —— the length.
el largo.
el LAHR-go.

541. —— **the width.**
el ancho.
el AHN-cho.

542. How long will it take?
¿Cuánto tardará?
KWAHN-toh tahr-dah-RAH?

543. Can you ship it to New York City?
¿Puede mandarlo a Nueva York?
PWAY-day mahn-DAHR-lo ah NWAY-vah york?

544. Do I pay [the salesgirl]?
¿Le pago [a la dependienta]?
lay PAH-go [ah lah day-pen-DYEN-tah]?

545. —— **the salesman.**
al dependiente.
ahl day-pen-DYEN-tay.

546. —— **the cashier.**
al cajero.
ahl kah-HAY-ro.

547. Please bill me.
Favor de cargarlo a mi cuenta.
fah-VOR day kahr-GAHR-lo ah mee KWEN-tah.

SHOPPING LIST

548. I want to buy [a bathing cap].
Quiero comprar [un gorro de baño].
KYAY-ro kohm-PRAHR [oon GO-rro day BAH-nyoh].

549. —— **a bathing suit.**
un traje de baño.
oon TRAH-hay day BAH-nyoh.

550. —— **a blouse.**
una blusa.
OO-nah BLOO-sah.

551. —— **a brassière.**
un sostén.
oon sohss-TEN.

552. —— **a topcoat.**
un abrigo.
oon ah-BREE-go.

553. —— **a dress.**
un vestido.
oon vess-TEE-doh.

554. —— **children's dresses.**
vestidos para niños.
vess-TEE-dohss PAH-rah NEE-nyohss.

555. —— **a pair of garters.**
un par de ligas.
oon pahr day LEE-gahss.

556. —— **a pair of gloves.**
un par de guantes.
oon pahr day GWAHN-tess.

557. —— **a handbag.**
una bolsa.
OO-nah BOHL-sah.

558. —— **one dozen handkerchiefs.**
una docena de pañuelos.
OO-nah doh-SAY-nah day pah-NWAY-lohss.

559. —— **a hat.**
un sombrero.
oon sohm-BRAY-ro.

560. —— **a jacket.**
una chaqueta.
OO-nah chah-KAY-tah.

561. —— **a nightgown.**
un camisón.
oon kah-mee-SOHN.

562. —— **a raincoat.**
un impermeable.
oon eem-payr-may-AH-blay.

563. —— **a pair of shoes.**
un par de zapatos.
oon pahr day sah-PAH-tohss.

564. —— **shoelaces.**
cintas de zapatos.
SEEN-tahss day sah-PAH-tohss.

565. —— **a skirt.**
una falda.
OO-nah FAHL-dah.

566. —— **a pair of slippers.**
un par de zapatillas.
oon pahr day sah-pah-TEE-yahss.

567. —— **a pair of socks.**
un par de calcetines.
oon pahr day kahl-say-TEE-ness.

568. —— **a pair of nylon stockings.**
un par de medias nylon.
oon pahr day MAY-dyahss nie-LOHN.

569. —— **a suit.**
un traje.
oon TRAH-hay.

570. —— **a sweater.**
un suéter.
oon SWAY-tayr.

571. —— **neckties.**
corbatas.
kor-BAH-tahss.

572. —— **a pair of trousers.**
un par de pantalones.
oon pahr day pahn-tah-LO-ness.

573. —— **underwear.**
      ropa interior.
      RRO-pah een-teh-RYOR.

574. **Do you have [ash trays]?**
      ¿Tiene [ceniceros]?
      TYAY-nay [say-nee-SAY-rohss]?

575. —— **artist's supplies.**
      material para artistas.
      mah-tay-RYAHL PAH-rah ahr-TEES-tahs.

576. —— **a box of candy.**
      una caja de dulces.
      OO-nah KAH-hah day DOOL-sayss.

577. —— **china.**
      loza.
      LOH-sah.

578. —— **a silver compact.**
      una polvera de plata.
      OO-nah pohl-VAY-rah day PLAH-tah.

579. —— **gold cuff links.**
      gemelos de oro.
      hay-MAY-lohss day O-ro.

580. —— **dolls.**
      muñecas.
      moo-NYAY-kahss.

581. —— **earrings.**
      aretes.
      ah-RAY-tayss.

582. —— **sheet music.**
      música para piano.
      MOO-see-kah PAH-rah PYAH-noh.

583. —— **musical instruments.**
      instrumentos musicales.
      een-stroo-MEN-tohss moo-see-KAH-layss.

584. —— **perfume.**
perfume.
payr-FOO-may.

585. —— **pictures.**
cuadros.
KWAH-drohss.

586. —— **records.**
discos.
DEES-kohss.

587. —— **silverware.**
platería.
plah-tay-REE-ah.

588. —— **souvenirs.**
recuerdos.
ray-KWEHR-dohss.

589. —— **toys.**
juguetes.
hoo-GAY-tayss.

590. —— **an umbrella.**
un paraguas.
oon pah-RAH-gwahss.

591. —— **a watch.**
un reloj.
oon rray-LOH.

COLORS

592. I want [a lighter shade].
Quiero [un tono más claro].
KYAY-ro [oon TOH-no mahss KLAH-ro].

593. —— **a darker shade.**
un tono más oscuro.
oon TOH-no mahss ohss-KOO-ro.

594. —— **black.**
negro.
NAY-gro.

595. —— **blue.**
azul.
ah-SOOL.

596. —— **brown.**
café.
kah-FAY.

597. —— **gray.**
gris.
greess.

598. —— **green.**
verde.
VAYR-day.

599. —— **orange.**
anaranjado.
ah-nah-rahn-HAH-doh.

600. —— **pink.**
rosado.
rro-SAH-doh.

601. —— **purple.**
morado.
mo-RAH-doh.

602. —— **red.**
rojo.
RRO-ho.

603. —— **white.**
blanco.
BLAHN-ko.

604. —— **yellow.**
amarillo.
ah-mah-REE-yoh.

STORES *

605. Where is [a bakery]?
¿Dónde hay [una panadería]?
DOHN-day I [OO-nah pah-nah-day-REE-ah]?

606. —— a candy store.
una dulcería.
OO-nah dool-say-REE-ah.

607. —— a cigar store.
una cigarrería.
OO-nah see-gah-rray-REE-ah.

608. —— a clothing store.
una tienda de ropa.
OO-nah TYEN-dah day RRO-pah.

609. —— a department store.
un almacén.
oon ahl-mah-SEN.

610. —— a drugstore.
una farmacia.
OO-nah fahr-MAH-syah.

611. —— a grocery.
una tienda de comestibles.
OO-nah TYEN-dah day ko-mess-TEE-blayss.

612. —— a hardware store.
una ferretería.
OO-nah fay-rray-tay-REE-ah.

613. —— a hat shop.
una sombrerería.
OO-nah sohm-bray-ray-REE-ah.

614. —— a jewelry store.
una joyería.
OO-nah ho-yay-REE-ah.

* Additional stores and services appear in the unrecorded section on Signs and Public Notices on page 106.

615. —— **a market.**
un mercado.
oon mayr-KAH-doh.

616. —— **a meat market.**
una carnicería.
OO-nah kahr-nee-say-REE-ah.

617. —— **a pastry shop.**
una panadería.
OO-nah pah-nah-day-REE-ah.

618. —— **a shoemaker.**
un zapatero.
oon sah-pah-TAY-ro.

619. —— **a shoe store.**
una zapatería.
OO-nah sah-pah-tay-REE-ah.

620. —— **a tailor shop.**
una sastrería.
OO-nah sahss-tray-REE-ah.

621. —— **a watchmaker.**
un relojero.
oon rray-lo-HAY-ro.

BOOKSTORE AND STATIONER'S

SIDE FIVE—BAND 3

622. **Where is there [a bookstore]?**
¿Dónde hay [una librería]?
DOHN-day I [OO-nah lee-bray-REE-ah]?

623. —— **a news dealer.**
un expendio de periódicos.
oon ess-PAYN-dyoh day pay-RYOH-dee-kohss.

624. —— **a stationer's.**
una papelería.
OO-nah pah-pay-lay-REE-ah.

625. I want to buy [a book].
Quiero comprar [un libro].
KYAY-ro kohm-PRAHR [oon LEE-bro].

626. —— **a guidebook.**
una guía.
OO-nah GHEE-ah.

627. —— **a dictionary.**
un diccionario.
oon deek-syoh-NAH-ryoh.

628. —— **a magazine.**
una revista.
OO-nah rray-VEESS-tah.

629. —— **a map of Mexico.**
un mapa de México.
oon MAH-pah day MAY-hee-ko.

630. —— **a newspaper.**
un periódico.
oon pay-RYOH-dee-koh.

631. I would like [some envelopes].
Quisiera [sobres].
kee-see-AY-rah [SO-bress].

632. —— **some ink.**
tinta.
TEEN-tah.

633. —— **some writing paper.**
papel para cartas.
pah-PEL PAH-rah KAHR-tahss.

634. —— **a fountain pen.**
una plumafuente.
OO-nah PLOO-mah-FWEN-tay.

635. —— **a pencil.**
un lápiz.
oon LAH-peess.

636. —— **some postcards.**
tarjetas postales.
tahr-HAY-tahss pohss-TAH-less.

637. —— **some wrapping paper.**
papel para envolver.
pah-PEL PAH-rah en-vohl-VAYR.

638. —— **some string.**
cuerda.
KWAYR-dah.

CIGAR STORE

639. **Where is the nearest cigar store?**
¿Dónde está la tabaquería más cercana?
*DOHN-day ess-TAH lah tah-bah-kay-REE-ah mahss
sayr-KAH-nah?*

640. **I want [some cigars].**
Deseo [unos puros].
day-SAY-o [OO-nohss POO-rohss].

641. —— **a pack of American cigarettes.**
un paquete de cigarrillos americanos.
*oon pah-KAY-tay day see-gah-RREE-yohss
ah-may-ree-KAH-nohss.*

642. —— **a leather cigarette case.**
una cigarrera de cuero.
OO-nah see-gah-RRAY-rah day KWAY-ro.

643. —— **a lighter.**
  un encendedor.
  oon en-sen-day-DOR.

644. —— **some pipe tobacco.**
  tabaco de pipa.
  tah-BAH-ko day PEE-pah.

645. **Do you have a match?**
  ¿Tiene un fósforo?
  TYAY-nay oon FOSS-fo-ro?

CAMERA SHOP

SIDE FIVE—BAND 4

646. **I want a roll of movie film for this camera.**
  Quiero un rollo de película de cine para esta cámara.
  KYAY-ro oon RRO-yo day pay-LEE-koo-lah day SEE-nay PAH-rah ESS-tah KAH-mah-rah.

647. **What is the charge for developing a roll of color film?**
  ¿Cuánto cuesta revelar un rollo de película de color?
  KWAHN-toh KWESS-tah rray-vay-LAHR oon RRO-yoh day pay-LEE-koo-lah day ko-LOHR?

648. **When will they be ready?**
  ¿Cuándo estarán listas?
  KWAHN-doh ess-tah-RAHN LEESS-tahss?

649. **May I take a snapshot of you?**
  ¿Me permite sacarle una foto?
  may payr-MEE-tay sah-KAHR-lay OO-nah FO-toh?

DRUGSTORE

650. Where is there a drugstore where they understand English?

¿Dónde hay una farmacia donde entiendan inglés?

DOHN-day I OO-nah fahr-MAH-syah DOHN-day ayn-TYEN-dahn een-GLAYSS?

651. Can you fill this prescription immediately?

¿Puede prepararme esta receta en seguida?

PWAY-day pray-pah-RAHR-may ESS-tah rray-SAY-tah en say-GHEE-dah?

652. Do you have [adhesive tape]?

¿Tiene [esparadrapo]?

TYAY-nay [ess-pah-rah-DRAH-po]?

653. —— alcohol.

alcohol.

ahl-KOHL.

654. —— antiseptic.

antiséptico.

ahn-tee-SEP-tee-ko.

655. —— aspirin.

aspirina.

ahss-pee-REE-nah.

656. —— an ice bag.

un saquito para hielo.

oon sah-KEE-toh PAH-rah YAY-lo.

657. —— a hairbrush.

un cepillo.

oon say-PEE-yoh.

658. —— a toothbrush.

un cepillo de dientes.

oon say-PEE-yoh day DYEN-tess.

659. —— **cold cream.**
crema para la cara.
KRAY-mah PAH-rah lah KAH-rah.

660. —— **a comb.**
un peine.
oon PAY-nay.

661. —— **corn pads.**
parches para callos.
PAHR-chess PAH-rah KAH-yohss.

662. —— **cotton.**
algodón.
ahl-go-DOHN.

663. —— **a deodorant.**
un desodorante.
oon dess-o-doh-RAHN-tay.

664. —— **cleaning fluid.**
quitamanchas.
kee-tah-MAHN-chahss.

665. —— **iodine.**
yodo.
YO-doh.

666. —— **a mild laxative.**
un laxante suave.
oon lak-SAHN-tay SWAH-vay.

•667. —— **lipstick.**
lápiz de labios.
LAH-peess day LAH-byohss.

668. —— **powder.**
polvos.
POHL-vohss.

669. —— **rouge.**
colorete.
ko-lo-RAY-tay.

670. —— **hairpins.**
horquillas.
or-KEE-yahss.

671. —— **a razor.**
una navaja de afeitar.
OO-nah nah-VAH-hah day ah-fay-TAHR.

672. —— **razor blades.**
hojas de afeitar.
O-hahss day ah-fay-TAHR.

673. —— **sanitary napkins.**
toallas higiénicas.
toh-AH-yahss ee-HYAY-nee-kahss.

674. —— **a sedative.**
un sedante.
oon say-DAHN-tay.

674. —— **shampoo.**
shampoo.
shahm-POO.

676. —— **a shaving lotion.**
una loción para después de afeitar.
OO-nah lo-SYOHN PAH-rah dess-PWAYSS day ah-fay-TAHR.

677. —— **(brushless) shaving cream.**
crema de afeitar (sin brocha).
KRAY-mah day ah-fay-TAHR (seen BRO-chah).

678. —— **sunglasses.**
lentes oscuros.
LEN-tess ohss-KOO-rohss.

679. —— **suntan oil.**
loción contra quemadura de sol.
lo-SYOHN KOHN-trah kay-mah-DOO-rah day sohl.

680. —— **a thermometer.**
un termómetro.
oon tayr-MO-may-tro.

681. —— **a tube of toothpaste.**
un tubo de pasta para los dientes.
oon TOO-bo day PAHSS-tah PAH-rah lohss DYEN-tess.

682. —— **toothpowder.**
polvo dentífrico.
POHL-vo den-TEE-free-ko.

LAUNDRY AND DRY CLEANING

SIDE SIX—BAND I

683. Where is [the laundry]?
¿Dónde está [la lavandería]?
DOHN-day ess-TAH [lah lah-vahn-day-REE-ah]?

684. —— **the dry cleaner?**
la tintorería?
lah teen-toh-ray-REE-ah?

685. I want these shirts [washed] mended.
Quiero que me [laven] remienden estas camisas.
KYAY-ro kay may [LAH-ven] rray-MYEN-den ESS-tahss kah-MEE-sahss.

686. Without starch.
Sin almidón.
seen ahl-mee-DOHN.

687. I want this suit [cleaned] pressed.
Quiero que me [limpien] planchen este traje.
KYAY-ro kay may [LEEM-pyen] PLAHN-chehn ESS-tay TRAH-hay.

688. The belt is missing.
Falta el cinturón.
FAHL-tah el seen-too-ROHN.

689. Can you sew on this button?
¿Puede coserme este botón?
PWAY-day ko-SAYR-may ESS-tay bo-TOHN?

690. Repair the zipper.
Compóngame el cierre.
kohm-POHN-gah-may el SYAY-rray.

BARBER SHOP AND BEAUTY PARLOR

691. Where is there [a good beauty parlor]?
¿Dónde hay [un buen salón de belleza]?
DOHN-day I [oon bwen sah-LOHN day bay-YAY-sah]?

692. —— a good barbershop.
una buena peluquería.
OO-nah BWEN-ah pay-loo-kay-REE-ah.

693. May I have a haircut, please?
Quiero una cortada de pelo, por favor.
KYAY-ro OO-nah kor-TAH-dah day PAY-lo, por fah-VOR?

694. Not too short.
No demasiado corto.
no day-mah-SYAH-doh KOR-toh.

695. No lotion, please.
No me ponga loción, por favor.
no may POHN-gah loh-SYOHN, por fah-VOR.

696. May I have [a shave]?
¿Me quiere dar [una afeitada]?
may KYAY-ray dahr [OO-nah ah-fay-TAH-dah]?

697. —— **a shampoo.**
un shampoo.
oon shahm-POO.

698. —— **a finger wave.**
un peinado al agua.
oon pay-NAH-doh ahl AH-gwah.

699. —— **a permanent.**
una permanente.
OO-nah payr-mah-NEN-tay.

700. —— **a manicure.**
un manicure.
oon mah-nee-KOO-ray.

701. —— **a facial.**
un masaje facial.
oon mah-SAH-hay fah-SYAHL.

702. —— **a massage.**
un masaje.
oon mah-SAH-hay.

703. —— **a shoeshine.**
una lustrada de zapatos.
OO-nah looss-TRAH-dah day sah-PAH-tohss.

HEALTH AND ILLNESS

SIDE SIX—BAND 2

704. I wish to see an American doctor.
Deseo ver a un médico norteamericano.
day-SAY-o vayr ah oon MAY-dee-ko nor-tay-ah-may-ree-KAH-no.

705. Is the doctor in?
¿Está el doctor?
ess-TAH el dok-TOHR?

706. I have [a headache].
Tengo [dolor de cabeza].
TEN-go [doh-LOHR day kah-BAY-sah].

707. —— **a cold.**
catarro.
kah-TAH-rro.

708. —— **a cough.**
tos.
tohss.

709. —— **constipation.**
estreñimiento.
ess-tray-nyee-MYEN-toh.

710. —— **diarrhoea.**
diarrea.
dyah-RRAY-ah.

711. —— **indigestion.**
indigestión.
een-dee-hess-TYOHN.

712. —— **fever.**
calentura.
kah-len-TOO-rah.

713. —— **nausea.**
náuseas.
NOW-say-ahss.

714. —— **a sore throat.**
inflamación de la garganta.
een-flah-mah-SYOHN day lah gahr-GAHN-tah.

715. There is something in my eye.
Tengo algo en el ojo.
TEN-go AHL-go en el O-ho.

716. I have a pain in my chest.
Tengo un dolor en el pecho.
TEN-go oon doh-LOHR en el PAY-cho.

717. I do not sleep well.
No duermo bien.
no DWAYR-mo byen.

718. Must I stay in bed?
¿Tengo que guardar cama?
TEN-go kay gwahr-DAHR KAH-mah?

719. When can I travel?
¿Cuándo puedo viajar?
KWAHN-doh PWAY-doh vyah-HAHR?

DENTIST

720. Do you know a good dentist?
¿Conoce a un buen dentista?
ko-NO-say ah oon bwen den-TEESS-tah?

721. This tooth hurts.
Me duele este diente.
may DWAY-lay ESS-tay DYEN-tay.

722. Can you fix it temporarily?
¿Puede usted componerlo por ahora?
PWAY-day oos-TED kohm-po-NAYR-lo por ah-O-rah?

723. I have lost a filling.
Perdí una tapadura.
payr-DEE OO-nah tah-pah-DOO-rah.

724. I do not want the tooth extracted.
No deseo que me saque el diente.
no day-SAY-o kay may SAH-kay el DYEN-tay.

TELEPHONING

SIDE SIX—BAND 3

725. Where can I telephone?
¿Dónde puedo telefonear?
DOHN-day PWAY-doh tay-lay-fo-nay-AHR?

726. Will you telephone for me?
¿Quiere telefonear de mi parte?
KYAY-ray tay-lay-fo-nay-AHR day mee PAHR-tay?

727. I want to make a local call, number 20-36-48.
Quiero hacer una llamada local, el número es el
veinte—treinta y seis—cuarenta y ocho.
*KYAY-ro ah-SAYR OO-nah yah-MAH-dah lo-
KAHL, el NOO-may-ro es el VAYN-tay—TRAYN-
tah ee sayss—kwah-REN-tah ee OH-cho.*

728. Give me the long-distance operator.
Comuníqueme con la operadora de larga distancia.
*ko-moo-NEE-kay-may kohn lah oh-pay-rah-DOH-rah
day LAHR-gah deess-TAHN-syah.*

729. My number is 20-28-67.
Hablo del veinte—veinte y ocho—sesenta y siete.
*AH-bloh del VAYN-tay—VAYN-tay ee OH-cho—
say-SEN-tah ee SYAY-tay.*

730. May I speak to Pedro?
¿Me permite hablar con Pedro?
may payr-MEE-tay ah-BLAHR kohn PAY-dro?

731. This is Carlos.
Habla Carlos.
AH-blah KAHR-lohss.

732. Please take a message for me.
Hágame el favor de tomar un mensaje.
*AH-gah-may el fah-VOHR day toh-MAHR oon
men-SAH-hay.*

AT THE POST OFFICE

(Conversation at normal rate of speech)

733. Quisiera mandar esta carta a los Estados Unidos. ¿Cuántos sellos lleva?

I'd like to send this letter to the United States. How many stamps does it take?

734. Por correo ordinario, veinte centavos. Por correo aéreo, cincuenta centavos por cada cinco gramos.

By regular mail, 20 centavos. By airmail, 50 centavos for each 5 grams.

735. Déme diez sellos de a veinte centavos y cinco de a cincuenta.

Give me ten 20-centavo stamps and five 50-centavo stamps.

736. Aquí los tiene. Cuatro pesos, cincuenta centavos, por favor.

Here they are. Four pesos and fifty centavos, please.

737. Muchas gracias. ¿Dónde puedo mandar este paquete por correo?

Thank you. Where can I send this package parcel post?

738. Yo puedo atenderlo. ¿Qué contiene?

I can take care of it. What does it contain?

739. Unos libros.

A few books.

740. ¿Son nuevos?

Are they new?

741. No. ¿Los puedo asegurar? ¿Cuánto cuesta el seguro?

No. Can I insure them? How much is the insurance?

742. Diez centavos por cada cincuenta pesos de seguro.

Ten centavos per 50 pesos of insurance.

743. Quisiera asegurarlos por veinte y cinco pesos.

I should like to insure them for 25 pesos.

744. Hágame el favor de llenar esta form. El importe total es de un peso, siete centavos — ochenta y dos centavos de correo y veinte y cinco centavos por el seguro.

Please fill out this form. The total charge is 1 peso, 7 centavos—82 centavos for postage and 25 centavos for insurance.

745. ¿Me da un recibo?

Will you give me a receipt?

746. Sí, señor. Hágame el favor de firmar aquí. A su derecha hay un buzón.

Yes, sir. Please sign your name here. To your right is a mail chute.

747. Muchas gracias.

Thanks very much.

SENDING A TELEGRAM

(Conversation at normal rate of speech)

748. Quisiera mandar un telegrama a Nueva York. ¿Cuánto cuesta por palabra?

I'd like to send a cablegram to New York City. What is the rate per word?

749. En un telegrama ordinario la tarifa es de diez y ocho centavos por palabra.

Regular cablegram is 18 centavos per word.

750. ¿Hay el mínimo corriente de diez palabras?
Is there the usual ten-word minimum?

751. No, señor, no hay un mínimo.
No, sir, there is no minimum charge.

752. ¿Se puede enviar una carta nocturna?
Can I send a night letter?

753. Sí. Cuesta la mitad pero se cobra un mínimo de veintidos palabras.
Yes, at a one-half rate, but there is a 22-word minimum charge.

754. ¿Cuándo llegaría una carta nocturna?
When would a night letter arrive?

755. Hasta mañana en la tarde.
Not until tomorrow afternoon.

756. ¿Cuándo llegaría un cable?
When would a cablegram arrive?

757. Dentro de cinco horas.
Within five hours.

758. Voy a mandar un cable ordinario. ¿Me permite unas formas?
I'll send a regular cablegram. May I have some forms?

759. Aquí las tiene. Tenga la bondad de escribir su nombre completo y su dirección en letras de imprenta. Una vez hecho esto, tendré mucho gusto en atenderle.
Here they are. Please print your full name and address. When you've done this, I'll be glad to take care of you.

760. Muchísimas gracias.
Thanks very much.

TIME AND TIME EXPRESSIONS

SIDE SIX—BAND 4

761. What time is it?
¿Qué hora es?
kay O-rah ess?

762. It is early.
Es temprano.
ess tem-PRAH-no.

763. It is (too) late.
Ya es (muy) tarde.
yah ess (mwee) TAHR-day.

764. It is two o'clock [A.M.].
Son las dos [de la mañana].
sohn lahss dohss [day lah mah-NYAH-nah].

765. —— P.M.
de la tarde.
day lah TAHR-day.

766. It is half-past three.
Son las tres y media.
sohn lahss trayss ee MAY-dyah.

767. It is quarter-past four.
Son las cuatro y cuarto.
sohn lahss KWAH-tro ee KWAHR-toh.

768. It is a quarter to five.
Son las cinco menos cuarto.
sohn lahss SEEN-ko MAY-nohss KWAHR-toh.

769. At ten minutes to six.
A las seis menos diez.
ah lahss sayss MAY-nohss dyess.

770. At twenty minutes past six.
A las seis y veinte.
ah lahss sayss ee VAYN-tay.

771. In the morning.
Por la mañana.
por lah mah-NYAH-nah.

772. In the afternoon.
Por la tarde.
por lah TAHR-day.

773. In the evening.
Por la noche.
por lah NO-chay.

774. Day.
El día.
el DEE-ah.

775. Night.
La noche.
lah NO-chay.

776. Last night.
Anoche.
ah-NO-chay.

777. Yesterday.
Ayer.
ah-YAYR.

778. Today.
Hoy.
oy.

779. Tonight.
Esta noche.
ESS-tah NO-chay.

780. Tomorrow.
Mañana.
mah-NYAH-nah.

781. Next week.
La semana próxima.
lah say-MAH-nah PROHK-see-mah.

DAYS OF THE WEEK

782. Monday.
Lunes.
LOO-ness.

783. Tuesday.
Martes.
MAHR-tess.

784. Wednesday.
Miércoles.
mee-AYR-ko-less.

785. Thursday.
Jueves.
HWAY-vess.

786. Friday.
Viernes.
vee-AYR-ness.

787. Saturday.
Sábado.
SAH-bah-doh.

788. Sunday.
Domingo.
doh-MEEN-go.

MONTHS AND SEASONS

789. January.
Enero.
ay-NAY-ro.

790. February.
Febrero.
fay-BRAY-ro.

791. March.
Marzo.
MAHR-so.

792. April.
Abril.
ah-BREEL.

793. May.
Mayo.
MAH-yoh.

794. June.
Junio.
HOO-nyoh.

795. July.
Julio.
HOO-lyoh.

796. August.
Agosto.
ah-GOHSS-toh.

797. September.
Septiembre.
sep-TYEM-bray.

798. October.
Octubre.
ok-TOO-bray.

799. November.
Noviembre.
no-VYEM-bray.

800. December.
Diciembre.
dee-SYEM-bray.

801. Spring.
La primavera.
lah pree-mah-VAY-rah.

802. Summer.
El verano.
el vay-RAH-no.

803. Autumn.
El otoño.
el o-TOH-nyoh.

804. Winter.
El invierno.
el een-vee-AYR-no.

805. Today is Friday, September first.
Hoy es viernes, primero de septiembre.
oy ess vee-AYR-ness, pree-MAY-ro day sep-TYEM-bray.

WEATHER

806. It is warm.
Hace calor.
AH-say kah-LOHR.

807. It is cold.
Hace frío.
AH-say FREE-o.

808. The weather is [good] bad.
Hace [buen] mal tiempo.
AH-say [bwen] mahl TYEM-po.

809. It is raining.
Llueve.
yoo-AY-vay.

NUMBERS

SIDE SIX—BAND 5

810. One. Uno. *OO-no.*
   Two. Dos. *dohss.*
   Three. Tres. *trayss.*
   Four. Cuatro. *KWAH-tro.*
   Five. Cinco. *SEEN-ko.*
   Six. Seis. *sayss.*
   Seven. Siete. *SYAY-tay.*
   Eight. Ocho. *O-cho.*
   Nine. Nueve. *NWAY-vay.*
   Ten. Diez. *dyess.*
   Eleven. Once. *OHN-say.*
   Twelve. Doce. *DOH-say.*
   Thirteen. Trece. *TRAY-say.*
   Fourteen. Catorce. *kah-TOR-say.*
   Fifteen. Quince. *KEEN-say.*
   Sixteen. Diez y seis. *dyess ee sayss.*
   Seventeen. Diez y siete. *dyess ee SYAY-tay.*
   Eighteen. Diez y ocho. *dyess ee O-cho.*
   Nineteen. Diez y nueve. *dyess ee NWAY-vay.*
   Twenty. Veinte. *VAYN-tay.*
   Twenty-one. Veintiuno. *vayn-tee-OO-no.*
   Twenty-two. Veintidós. *vayn-tee-DOHSS.*
   Thirty. Treinta. *TRAYN-tah.*
   Thirty-one. Treinta y uno. *TRAYN-tah ee OO-no.*
   Forty. Cuarenta. *kwah-REN-tah.*
   Fifty. Cincuenta. *seen-KWEN-tah.*
   Sixty. Sesenta. *say-SEN-tah.*

Seventy. Setenta. *say-TEN-tah.*

Seventy-one. Setenta y uno. *say-TEN-tah ee OO-no.*

Eighty. Ochenta. *o-CHEN-tah.*

Eighty-one. Ochenta y uno. *o-CHEN-tah ee OO-no.*

Ninety. Noventa. *no-VEN-tah.*

Ninety-one. Noventa y uno. *no-VEN-tah ee OO-no.*

Ninety-two. Noventa y dos. *no-VEN-tah ee dohss.*

One hundred. Cien. *syen.*

Two hundred. Doscientos. *dohss-SYEN-tohss.*

Five hundred. Quinientos. *kee-NYEN-tohss.*

Seven hundred. Setecientos. *say-tay-SYEN-tohss.*

Nine hundred. Novecientos. *no-vay-SYEN-tohss.*

One thousand. Mil. *meel.*

Two thousand. Dos mil. *dohss meel.*

One million. Un millón. *oon mee-LYOHN.*

SIGNS AND PUBLIC NOTICES
(Not recorded, and alphabetized in Spanish)

This list includes most of the recurring signs and notices that one sees on the streets and in public places. There is no need to memorize this list now, but do review it when you arrive in a foreign city. If you plan to drive, the study of road signs on page 112 is imperative. With the help of this list or a pocket dictionary, make an effort to learn the meaning of common signs you see. It is an excellent way to build your vocabulary in the course of your travels, because signs and notices, by and large, reflect the current language that answers everyday practical needs. You will also find that when you understand almost all the common signs you see around you, you will be more at home and confident in your new environment.

Abajo. Down.
Abierto de . . . a . . . Open from . . . to . . .
Abogado. Lawyer.
Agencia de empleos. Employment agency.
Agencia de boletos. Ticket office.
Agente de bolsa. Stockbroker.
Agente de noticias. News agent.
Agente de viajes. Travel agent.
Aire acondicionado. Air-conditioned.
A la (izquierda) derecha. To the (left) right.
Al (barco) tren. To the (boat) train.
Al detalle. Retail.
Almuerzo. Lunch.
Al por mayor. Wholesale.
Anuncio público. Public notice.
Apague la luz. Turn off the lights.
Aquí se habla inglés. English spoken here.
Arriba. Up.

Ascensor. Elevator.
Asiento reservado. Reserved seat.
Autos de uso. Used cars.
Avisos. Signs.
Ayuntamiento. City hall.

Banco. Bank.
Banco de ahorros. Savings bank.
Bar. Bar.
Barbería. Barbershop.
Basura. Rubbish.
Biblioteca. Library.
Bicicletas. Bicycles.
Bienes raíces. Real estate.
Billar. Billiards.
Bolos. Bowling.
Buffet. Buffet.
Buzón. Mail box.

Caballeros. Men; gentlemen.
Cafetería. Coffee shop.
Caliente. Hot.
Cambio de moneda. Money exchanged.
Carga. Trucking.
Carnicero. Butcher.
Cementerio. Cemetery.
Cerrado de . . . a . . . Closed from . . . to . . .
Cerrado domingos y días festivos. Closed on
  Sundays and holidays.
Cerveza. Beer.
Cine. Movies.
Clínica. Hospital.
Coche comedor. Dining car.
Comedor. Dining room.
Corredor. Broker.

Correos. Post office.
Cosméticos. Cosmetics.
Costurera. Dressmaker.
Cuarto de baño. Bathroom; toilet.
Cuidado. Look out; watch your step.
Cuidado con el perro. Beware of the dog.

Dentista. Dentist.
Deposite . . . centavos. Deposit . . . centavos.

Efectos deportivos. Sporting goods.
Efectos eléctricos. Electrical appliances.
Efectos para el hogar. Household wares.
Empleados. Employees only.
Empuje. Push.
Encargado. Janitor.
Entrada. Entrance.
Entrada gratis. Admission free.
Entre. Enter.
Escaleras. Stairs.
Escuela comercial. Business school.
Estación. Depot.
Estacionamiento gratis. Free parking.
Estación de ferrocarril. Railroad station.
Estudio de baile. Dance studio.
Exportador. Exporter.
Expreso. Express.

Fábrica. Factory.
Ficha. Token.
Florería. Flower shop.
Fotógrafo. Photographer.
Frío. Cold.
Frutería. Fruit store.
Fumador. Smoking car.

Funeraría. Funeral parlor.
Función continua. Continuous performance.

Galería de arte. Art gallery.
Gangas. Bargains.
Guardarropía. Checkroom.
Guardián. Caretaker.

Helados. Ices.
Hombres trabajando. Men at work.
Hospital. Hospital.

Importador. Importer.
Imprenta. Printing.
Información. Information.
Intérprete. Interpreter.

Jardín botánico. Botanical garden.
Jardín zoológico. Zoo.

Lavandería y tintbrería. Laundry and dry cleaner.
Letreros. Signs.
Libre. Vacant.
Librero. Bookseller.
Limpiabotas. Bootblack.
Llegada. Arrival.

Madera. Lumber.
Máquinas de coser. Sewing machines.
Merendero. Snack bar.
Mesa reservada. Table reserved.
Modisto. Couturier.
Motocicletas. Motorcycles.
Muebles. Furniture.
Museo. Museum.

No dé de comer a los animales.   Do not feed the animals.
No hay función.   No performance.
No pise el césped.   Keep off the grass.
No ruidos.   No noise.

Oculista.   Oculist.
Ocupado.   Engaged.
¡Ojo!   Watch out!

Pase.   Enter.
Peatones.   Pedestrians.
Peligro.   Danger.
Peligro de incendio.   Danger of fire.
Pintor de letreros.   Sign painter.
Pintura.   Paints.
Pintura fresca.   Wet paint.
Panadería.   Bakery.
Parada de ómnibus.   Bus stop.
Policía.   Police.
Precio de entrada.   Admission.
Préstamos.   Loans.
Prohibido el paso.   No trespassing.
Prohibido escupir en el suelo.   No spitting.
Prohibido fumar.   No smoking.
Prohibida la entrada (excepto para asuntos de negocios).   No admittance (except on business).
Prohibido nadar.   No swimming.
Propiedad privada (particular).   Private property.

Radios.   Radios.
Refrescos.   Refreshments.
Regalos.   Gifts.
Reparaciones.   Auto repairs.
Ropa para caballeros.   Men's clothing.
Ropa para señora.   Ladies' clothing.

Sala de espera.　Waiting room.
Salida.　Departure; exit.
Salida de emergencia.　Emergency exit.
Salón de belleza.　Beauty parlor.
Sastre.　Tailor.
Se alquila esta casa.　House for rent.
Se alquilan autos.　Auto rentals.
Se alquilan habitaciones amuebladas.　Furnished rooms to let.
Se (alquila) vende.　For (hire, rent) sale.
Se lustran zapatos.　Shoes shined.
Señoras.　Ladies.
Se permite fumar.　Smoking allowed.
Se prohibe nadar (bañarse).　Bathing not allowed.
Se prohiben bicicletas.　No bicycles allowed.
Se solicita ...　You are requested to ...
Se vende aquí.　On sale here.
Silencio (por favor).　Quiet (please).
Sitio de taxis.　Taxi stand.
Sombrerería.　Millinery.

Tabaquería.　Tobacco shop.
Tapizador.　Upholsterer.
Teléfono público.　Public telephone.
Televisión.　Television.
Tienda de animales.　Pet shop.
Tienda de comestibles.　Grocery.
Tire.　Pull.
Toque el timbre.　Ring bell.

Ultramarinos.　Delicatessen.

Veneno. Para uso externo.　Poison.　For external use.
Vinos y licores.　Wines and liquors.

ROAD SIGNS

Acelere de nuevo. Resume speed.
Altura límite. Clearance.
Altura máxima. Maximum clearance.

Bache. Bump.

Callejón sin salida. Dead end.
Cambie de vía. Change lane.
Cambie velocidad. Change gear.
Camino (calle) de una vía. One-way (street) road.
Camino cerrado. Road closed.
Camino estrecho. Narrow road.
Camino (carretera) en malas condiciones. Bad road; road in poor condition.
Camino particular. Private road.
Camino principal. Main road.
Carga máxima. Weight limit.
Carretera de primera clase (adelante). Major road (ahead).
Carretera en reparación. Road repairs.
Conduzca con cuidado. Drive carefully.
Cruce. Crossroads.
Cruce de arteria (vía) principal. Crossing main thoroughfare.
Cruce de ferrocarril (con) sin barreras. Railroad crossing (with) without gates.
Cruce de nivel (con barreras). Level crossing (with gates).
Cruce de peatones. Pedestrian crossing.
Curva (peligrosa). (Dangerous) curve.
Curva cerrada. Sharp turn.
Cuidado. Caution.
¡Cuidado! En construcción. Caution! Road construction ahead.

¡Cuidado! Tranvía. Caution! Tramway.
Curva doble. Double curve.

Derrumbe de rocas. Fallen rock.
Descenso. Dip.
Deslizamiento de rocas. Fallen rock.
Despacio. Escuela. Drive slowly. School.
Desvío. Detour.
Disminuya velocidad. Slow down.
Doble a la derecha. Turn right.

Entrada. Entrance; entry.
Escuela. School.
Estación de primeros auxilios. First-aid station.

Ferry. Ferry.

Hielo. Ice.
Hombres trabajando. Men working.
Hospital. Hospital.

Intersección. Intersection.

Línea de parada. Stop line.

Maneje con cuidado. Drive with caution.
Maneje despacio. Drive slowly.
Mantenga (su derecha) su izquierda. Keep (right) left.

Pare. Stop.
Pase a la (derecha) izquierda de este aviso. Pass to the (right) left of this sign.
Pase con cuidado. Pass with caution.
Paso inferior. Underpass.

Peligro. Danger.
Pendiente. Steep grade.
Prohibido detenerse. No stopping.
Prohibido dar vuelta. No turns.
Prohibido (el paso de) motocicletas. Motorcycles prohibited.
Prohibido el paso de vehículos. Closed to all vehicles.
Prohibido el tránsito de automoviles. Automobiles prohibited.
Prohibido estacionarse. No parking.
Prohibido parar. Siga adelante. Do not stop. Keep going.
Prohibido pasar. No passing
Propiedad privada. Private property.
Puente levadizo. Drawbridge.

Reduzca velocidad. Reduce speed.
Resbalosa cuando mojada. Slippery when wet.
Ruta número. Route number.

Salida. Exit.
Se prohibe dar vuelta a la (derecha) izquierda. No (right) left turn.
Servicio sanitario. Rest rooms.

NATIVE FOOD AND DRINK LIST

This food supplement consists mainly of native Spanish dishes. We have however also included a selection of Latin American, South American and Mexican dishes; all of which show strong Spanish influence. All foods have been alphabetized according to Spanish to facilitate menu reading. Typical and standard American foods can be found in the restaurant section of the text.

Note that dining hours in Spain, Latin and South America are distinctly later than they are in the United States. Breakfast is simple, usually rolls and coffee served between 8–11 a.m. Lunch is leisurely and substantial; usually served between 1–3 o'clock and always followed by a siesta. Dinner or supper is customarily served after 9 p.m. and more likely after 10 o'clock. The custom of stopping at 5 o'clock for cocktails or coffee and a snack is very characteristic of Spanish life. It is typical of Spanish night life to begin extremely late and to continue far into the night.

SOPAS: SOUPS
APERTIVOS: APPETIZERS

Calderada. Fish soup; a variety of bouillabaisse.

Caldo. Chicken broth.

Caldo de pimentón. Pepper soup.

Entremeses. Hors d'œuvres.

Espárragos. Large, succulent asparagus.

Fondos de alcachofas. Hearts of artichokes with oil and vinegar.

Gazpacho. Chilled vegetable soup made with cucumbers, tomatoes, red pepper, onions, garlic, bread crumbs, oil and vinegar.

Potaje de garbanzos. Pea soup made with chick peas.

Potaje de habas secas. Bean soup made with dried beans.

Salmorejo. Chilled vegetable soup similar to Gazpacho.

Sancochas de camerones. Shrimp chowder.

Sopa de Agriao. Potato and watercress soup.

Sopa de ajo. Garlic soup usually served with a poached egg.

Sopa de ajo blanco. Cold soup made of melon or grapes.

Sopa de albóndigas. Soup with meat balls made with a tomato base and served with small fried meat balls in it.

Sopa de almendras. Purée of almond soup.

Sopa de camarones. Shrimp soup.

Sopa de coles. Cabbage soup.

Sopa de cuarto de hora. Fish soup made of fish and shell fish and served with hard boiled eggs, peas and toasted bread.

Sopa de galápagos. Turtle soup.
Sopa de legumbres. Vegetable soup.
Sopa de mariscos. Seafood soup.
Sopa de ostras. Oyster soup.
Sopa de pan con gambas. Bread soup with prawns.
Sopa de pescado. Fish soup prepared with one kind of fish or a variety of native fish.
Sopa de puchero. Thick beef soup.
Sopa de rana. Frog soup.
Sopa de tomate. Tomato soup.
Sopa de verduras. Vegetable soup.
Sopa española. Soup made with rice, tomatoes, peppers and spices.
Tapas. Small snacks taken with sherry or vermouth before meals consisting of olives, almonds, cheese, fish, anchovies.

PESCADO: FISH
MARISCOS: SHELLFISH

Abadejo. Cod.
Alli-pebre d'anguiles. Eel in garlic sauce.
Almejas. Clams.
Almejas con arroz. Clams and rice.
Anguilas. Eels.
Arenques. Herring.
Atún. Tuna fish.
Atún en escabeche. Pickled tuna.
Bacalao. Dried cod fish.
Besugo. Sea bream.
Bogavante. Lobster.
Bonito. Bonito.

Boquerones.   Fish, very much like anchovies.
Caballa.   Mackerel.
Caldereta asturiana.   Mixed fish stew.
Callos.   Tripe.
Calmares.   Squid.
Calmares en su tinta.   Small cuttlefish simmered in their own ink.
Camarones.   Shrimps.
Cangrejos.   Crabs.
Caracoles.   Snails.
Chanquetes.   Small, thin fried fish.
Chocos con habas.   Cuttlefish with broad beans.
Chupe.   Thick fish stew.
Coquines.   Cockles.
Escabeche.   Pickled fish.
Gambas.   Large shrimp.
Huachinango.   Red snapper.
Lamprea.   Lamprey.
Langosta.   Variety of lobster.
Langostinos.   Shellfish (crayfish) similar to shrimp.
Lenguado.   Sole.
Lentejas con chorizo.   Lentils and sausage.
Lisa.   Grey mullet.
Llobarro, grillé o hervido.   Sea bass, grilled or boiled.
Mariscos.   Shellfish.
Marmita.   Fish stew in which bonito is predominant.
Mejillones.   Mussels.
Merluza.   Codfish.
Mitulo rellenos.   Stuffed mussels.
Ostras.   Oysters.
Paella.   Popular Spanish dish prepared with chicken, shellfish, sausage, pimento and saffron-flavored rice.
Paella de mariscos.   Rice and seafood.

Pargo encebollado.   Red bream baked with onions.
Perca.   Perch.
Pescado blanco en ajillo.   White fish with garlic.
Pescado con arroz.   Fish with rice.
Pescado con salsa de coconut.   Fish with a coconut sauce.
Pez espada en amarillo.   Swordfish cooked with herbs.
Raya en pimentón.   Skate and red pepper.
Róbalo.   Bass.
Rodaballo.   Flounder.
Rollo de pescado.   Fish roll.
Sábalo.   Shad.
Salmón.   Salmon.
Salmonetes.   Baby salmon.
Sardinas.   Sardines.
Trucha.   Trout.
Zarzuela.   Mixture of seafoods prepared in a spicy sauce.

CARNE: MEAT   AVES: POULTRY
ESPECIALIDADES: SPECIALTIES

Ajiaco.   Meat, chicken, pepper, avocado and potatoes prepared in a stew.
Ajoqueso.   Latin American dish of melted cheese and peppers.
Albondigón.   Meat loaf.
Arroz con pollo.   Chicken with rice.
Arroz a la parellada.   Rice prepared with chicken, meat and vegetables.
Biftec or bistec.   Steak.
Berenjena rellena.   Stuffed eggplant.

Butifarra. Pork sausage.

Cabeza de ternera. Calf's head with vinaigrette sauce.

Cabrito asado. Roast leg of spring lamb.

Caldo gallego. Thick stew of meat and vegetables.

Cazuela de cordero. Lamb stew made with corn, peas, beans, rice, potatoes and herbs.

Cebollas y frijoles. Bean-stuffed onions.

Chanfaina. Goat entrails with vegetables.

Chile con carne. Highly seasoned ground beef, beans and chile in a spicy sauce.

Chile con queso. Highly seasoned chili (peppers) and cheese.

Cholupas. Spicy Mexican dish prepared with sausage, chili and onions.

Chorizo. Garlic and pork sausage.

Chuletas de cerdo. Pork cutlets.

Chuletas de cordero. Lamb cutlets.

Chuletas de ternera. Veal cutlets.

Cocido. Boiled meat with ham, bacon, sausage and vegetables.

Cochinillo asado. Roast suckling pig.

Codornices asadas. Roast quail.

Cola de vaca. Oxtail.

Conejo. Rabbit.

Cordero en ajillo pastor. Lamb stew.

Corona de cordero. Crown of lamb.

Costillas de cerdo. Spareribs.

Costillas de cordero a la parrilla. Grilled lamb chops.

Croqueta de pollo. Chicken croquettes.

Croquetas de papas con carne. Meat and potato cakes.

Empanadas. Meat pies.

Empanadillas. Small pastries filled with meat.

Enchiladas. Mexican corn cake stuffed with meat, cheese and chile.

Estofado. Stew made with diced chicken, beef, lamb, ham, onions, tomatoes, herbs and wine.

Fabada asturiana. Pork and beans.

Frijolada. Bean stew with meat and native vegetables.

Frijoles. Beans with bacon and ham.

Fritos de lentejas. Fried lentils.

Fritura mixta. Assorted meat, chicken or fish and vegetables, fried in deep fat.

Gallina. Chicken.

Gallina con garbanzos. Stewed chicken with chick peas.

Guacamole. Finely chopped onions, spices and avocados.

Guisado español. Stew made with beef, onions in olive oil.

Hígado de ternera a la parrilla. Grilled calf's liver.

Humita. Pancake made with fresh corn, tomato, pimento, sugar and oil.

Ignames con ron. Sweet potatoes prepared with rum and sherry.

Jamón. Ham of the region.

Jamón aguadilla. Roast fresh ham.

Jamón serrano. Smoked ham.

Jigote. Meat hash.

Locro. Corn stew made with wheat, meat and spices; popular in South America.

Lomo a la parrilla. Grilled pork chops.

Longaniza. Pork sausage.

Medallones con champiñones. Filet of beef or veal with mushrooms.

Menudo gitana. Well seasoned tripe.

Mole de guajalote. Mexican dish made with chicken, garlic, onions, tomatoes, tortillas in a chocolate sauce.

Mole poblano. Chicken or turkey exotically seasoned and prepared in a chocolate sauce.

Mondongo. Thick stew prepared with many native vegetables.

Morcilla blanca. Sausage made with chicken, bacon, hard boiled eggs and spices.

Morcilla asturiana. Blood sausage.

Olla podrida. Stew made with ham and chick peas.

Paella. Native Spanish dish prepared with chicken, seafood, sausage, onions, garlic, tomatoes, pimento and saffron flavored rice.

Pato con cereza. Braised duck with cherry sauce.

Pato silvestre. Wild duck.

Pavo asado. Roast turkey.

Pecho de ternera. Breast of veal.

Pelota. Chopped beef.

Pepitoria de gallina. Chicken stew made with olives, tomatoes and vegetables.

Perdices asadas. Roast partridge.

Perdiz. Partridge.

Perdiz en escabeche. Marinated partridge.

Picadillo. Hash.

Pichones. Squabs, pigeons.

Pie de cerdo bretóna. Pigs knuckles with beans.

Pierna de cordero. Leg of lamb.

Pimientos rellenos. Stuffed peppers.

Pisto manchego. Stew made with onions, eggs and pork.

Pollo asado frío con ensalada. Chicken salad.

Pollo con naranja. Chicken prepared with an orange sauce.

Pote gallego. Stew prepared with beef, ham sausage and vegetables.

Puchero. Boiled dinner made of meat and vegetables.

Puerco estofado. Spicy, pork stew.

Redondo asado. Roast veal.

Riñones. Kidneys.

Riñones al jerez. Kidneys prepared in a sauce of sherry.

Rollo de Santiago. Meat loaf covered with potatoes.

Ropa vieja. Meat hash.

Rosbif. Roast beef.

Salchichas. Veal and pork sausage (always eaten fresh).

Salchichón. Pork and bacon sausage.

Salpicón de ave. Chicken with mayonnaise.

Sancocho. Stew of meat, yucca and bananas.

Sesos. Brains.

Simplón frito. Fried noodles.

Solomillo. Filet of veal.

Suculento. Vegetable dish prepared with corn, squash and other native vegetables.

Tallarines. Noodles.

Tamale. A mixture of ground corn filled with minced chicken or meat and steamed or fried in oil.

Ternera asada fría. Cold roast veal.

Torta de conejo. Rabbit tart.

Tortas de carne. Meat patties.

Tortilla, Mexican. A thin, flat unleavened corn cake.

Tortilla, Spanish. An omelet.

Tortilla con jamón. Ham omelet.

Tortilla española. Spanish omelet.

Totilla de sardinas. Sardine omelet.

Tostón asado. Roast suckling pig.

Tasajo. Corned beef.

ENSALADAS: SALADS

Ensalada de pepino.   Cucumber salad.
Ensalada de tomate.   Tomato salad.
Ensalada variada.   Mixed green salad.

POSTRES: DESSERTS

Alfajores.   Filled cookies.
Almendrado.   Macaroon.
Arroz con leche.   Rice with milk.
Bizcochitos.   Crackers, cookies.
Bizcochuelo.   Cake.
Budín.   Pudding.
Buñuelos.   Doughnuts.
Cabello de ángel.   Jam made from a gourd, called sidra.
Capirotada.   Sweet pudding made with bread and cinnamon.
Carne de membrillo.   Preserved quince.
Churros.   Light pastry dough rolled into long, thin strips, fried and rolled in sugar.
Compota.   Stewed fruit.
Crema española.   Dessert made of eggs, milk and gelatin.
Cuajada.   Junket.
Flan.   Caramel custard; a classic Spanish dessert.
Flan cremoso.   Boiled custard.
Gelatina.   Gelatin.
Guayaba.   Guava.
Helados.   Ice cream.
Higo en almíbar.   Figs in syrup.
Magdalenas.   Little cakes.
Mantecado.   Ice cream.

Mantecadas de almendras.   Almond biscuits.
Masitas.   Cupcakes.
Mazapán.   Marzipan.
Membrillo.   Jellied dessert made of quinces.
Melón.   Melon.
Merengue.   Meringue.
Migas.   Fried bread.
Mostachones.   Little cakes eaten at festivities.
Natilla.   Custard.
Pastas.   Pastry.
Pasteles.   Cakes.
Pastelitos.   Small cakes.
Perruñas.   Little biscuits.
Piña.   Pineapple.
Pudín.   Pudding.
Roscas.   Cookies.
Rosquillas.   Biscuits shaped in the form of rings.
Sandía.   Watermelon.
Sorbete.   Sherbet.
Suspiros.   Little fried cakes sprinkled with sugar.
Tarta.   Tart, pie.
Tarteletas.   Small tarts.
Torta.   Cake.
Torta de almendras.   Almond tart.
Tortera.   Pastry.
Turrón.   Nougat dessert.
Yemas.   Candy dessert made with egg yolks, sugar, fruits, nuts; formed into small balls.

QUESOS: CHEESES

Cabrales.   Somewhat like blue cheese.
Manchego.   Spanish cheese made with ewe's milk.
Queso de bola.   Cheese made from cow's milk and eaten fresh similar to Dutch edam.

Queso de cabra. Goat's milk cheese.
Queso gallego. Medium soft cheese.
Requesón. Soft, white cheese similar to cottage cheese.

BEBIDAS: DRINKS

Anís. Anise.
Aperitivo. Aperitif.
Cerveza. Beer.
Champaña. Champagne.
Chicha. Fermented maize or pineapple drink.
Coñac. Brandy.
Gaseosa. Soda.
Ginebra. Gin.
Guarapo. Cider.
Jerez. Sherry.
Oporto. Port.
Ponche. Punch.
Pulque. Strong, fermented drink made from the Mexican maquay plant.
Ron. Rum.
Sidra. Cider.
Vino. Wine.
  Vino blanco. White wine.
  Vino de Borgoña. Burgundy wine.
  Vino de Burdeos. Bordeaux wine.
  Vino corriente. Ordinary table wine.
  Vino de cuarte. Pink wine.
  Vino spumoso. Sparkling wine.
  Vino de la tierra. Regional wine.
  Vino tinto. Red wine.

INDEX

The numbers following all Index entries refer to *item numbers*, except for major section entries which are in capitals and refer to *page number*.

Accelerator 250
address 29, 759
adhesive tape 652
adjust 242
afternoon 772, 755
again 30
agent 131
ahead, straight 154
air-conditioned 270
airline office 130
airmail 734
AIRPLANE p. 39
airport 192
à la carte 331
alcohol 653
all 115, 122
all right 21, 71
all, that is 73
A.M. 764, 290
American 37, 107, 641, 704

AMUSE-MENTS p. 70
anchovies 396
another 320, 472
antiseptic 654
anyone 51
apartment 265
appetite 364
apple 434
appointment 5
April 792
architecture 484
are 740
arrival 199
arrive 133, 754
artist's supplies 575
ash tray 574
asparagus 414, 463
aspirin 655
assorted 471
at 152
August 796
aunt 27

AUTOMO-BILE TRAVEL p. 43
autumn 803
avenue 212

Back (*adv.*) 161
bacon 392
bad 230, 808
bag 113
BAGGAGE p. 32
baggage 109, 124
— check 126
— room 125
baked potato 429, 463
bakery 605
balcony 280
bank 520
BANK AND MONEY p. 73
BARBER SHOP p. 91
bartender 310

bath 277
— mat 300
bathing cap 548
— suit 549
battery 239, 251
be 266
beach 510
beans 415
BEAUTY PARLOR p. 91
because 474
bed 275, 718
beef 397, 398, 460, 461
beer 318
before 456
begin 464
behind 158
bellhop 289
belt 688
best 262
better 531
BEVERAGES p. 65
bill (*n.*) 307, 360
bill (*v.*) 547
black 594
black coffee 444, 472
blanket 294
blouse 550

blue 595
boarding house 264
board, on 179
BOAT p. 38
boiled 347
— potato 427
Bon Voyage! 180
book 625, 739
BOOK-STORE p. 83
bookstore 622
bottle 312, 457
box (receptacle) 576
box (loge) 504
box office 499
boy 75
brake 242
brassière 551
bread 368
breakfast 291, 323
BREAKFAST FOODS p. 59
bring 294, 333, 472
broiled chicken 399
broken 102
brother 13
brown 596

brushless shaving cream 677
bullfight 511
BUS p. 41
bus 212
— service 192
— stop 209
business man 41
— section 135
— trip 43
but (except) 118
butter 369
button 689
buy 548, 625

Cabbage 416
cabin 184
cablegram 748, 756
CAFÉ, AT THE, p. 52
cake 449
call (summon) 217, 290
call (visit) 30
call (*n.*) 727
Camembert cheese 471
camera 646
CAMERA SHOP p. 86

can I 164, 178,
741
can you 95,
103, 244, 322
candy 576
— store 606
captain 181
car 225, 240
carefully 128,
222
carrot 417
cash (v.) 521,
522
cashier 546
castle 487
cathedral 488
Catholic 479
catsup 376
cauliflower 418
celery 419
center of town
266
cereal 383
certificate 112
chair 186
chambermaid
288
champagne 316
change (coins)
527
change (ex-
change) 238,
357, 525
change (trans-
fer) 214

charge 219,
483, 647,
744
cheaper 532
check (bank)
522, 523
check (bill)
358, 474
check (exam-
ine) 243
check baggage
124
cheese 451, 471
cherry 435
chest 716
chicken 399,
400
— soup 394,
465
child 16
children's
dresses 554
china 577
chocolate 454,
471
choose 462
Christmas 35
CHURCH
p. 69
church 479
cigar 640
CIGAR
STORE
p. 85

cigar store 639,
607
cigarette 641
— case 642
— lighter 643
circle 213
citizen 37
city 137
class 170
clean (adj.)
353, 472
clean (v.) 241,
687
cleaning fluid
664
close (v.) 203,
490
clothing 118
— store 608
clutch 252
cocktail 311
coffee, 444, 468
cognac 315
cold (adj.) 47,
354, 807
cold (n.) 707
cold cream 659
color film 647
COLORS
p. 80
comb 660
come 28, 193
— back 293
— here 90
— in 91

compact 578
concert 493
condition 230
congratulations 32
constipation 709
consulate 107
contain 738
cooked 345, 383
cookies 452
corner 152
corn pads 661
cotton 662
cough 708
cover charge 507
cream 445
cucumber 420
cuff links 579
cup 444
custard 452
CUSTOMS p. 30
customs 108

Dance 506
dark beer 318
darker 593
daughter 9
day, 282, 774
DAYS OF THE WEEK p. 101

December 800
deck 185
— chair 186
declare 114
DENTIST p. 94
dentist 720
deodorant 663
department store 609
departure 200
dessert 469, 471
DESSERTS p. 65
develop 647
diarrhoea 710
dictionary 627
DIFFICULTIES p. 29
dine 331
diner 204
dinner 322, 468
direct way 134
do, what am I to 101
dock 188
doctor 704, 705
doll 580
dollar 524, 526
double bed 275
double room 272
downstairs 284
dozen 558
dramamine 190

dress 553, 554
drink 310
drinking water 365
drive 221, 222
driver 215
driver's license 226
DRUGSTORE p. 87
drugstore 650, 610
dry cleaner 684
DRY CLEANING p. 90
duck 401
dutiable 120

Early 762
earrings 581
east 142
eat 178
eggs 387
eight 810
eighteen 810
eighty 810
eighty-one 810
elevator 285
eleven 810
empty 236
engine 247
English 50, 482, 650

English-speaking 476
enjoy 26
enough 352
entrance 491
ENTRÉES p. 60
equivalent 526
evening 773
—performance 501
everything 116, 129, 308
excellent 363
excess 196
exchange rate 524
excuse me 68
exit 492
express (train) 174
extract 724
eye 715
eyeglasses 102

Facial massage 701
family 23
far 162, 163
fat 342
father 15
February 790
fever 712
few, a 739

fifteen 810
fifty 810
filet of sole 460
fill (prescription) 651
filling 723
fill out 744
film 646, 647
find 97
fine 19
finger wave 698
finish 123
first class 170
fish 402
fishing 516
five 810
fix (repair) 244, 722
flat tire 244
flight 194
floor show 501
food 341, 363
FOOD LIST p. 57
for 193, 726, 274
forget 99
form 758
fork 336
forty 810
forward (adv.) 160
forward (v.) 309

fountain pen 634
four 810
four-minute eggs 388
fourteen 810
free 218
Friday 786
fried 346
— chicken 400
— eggs 390
— onions 463
— potatoes 430
friend 11, 42, 96
from 201
front, in 159
fruit cup 465
— juice 379
FRUITS p. 62
full 236
furnished apartment 265

Garage 228
garlic 375, 467
garters 555
gasoline 235
gas station 227
gear shift 253
get off 215, 216

gift 119
girl 76
give (present) 29, 237, 330
give (connect) 728
glad 48, 759
glass 313, 446
glove 556
go 130, 132, 165, 474, 493, 506, 510, 516, 528
gold 579
golf 515
good (competent) 720
good (first-class) 230, 460, 808
good-bye 3
good evening 2
good morning 1
goose 403
gram 734
grape 437
grapefruit 436
gray 597
green 598
GREETINGS AND SOCIAL CONVERSATION p. 19

grocery 611
guide 482
guidebook 626

Hairbrush 657
haircut 693
hairpin 670
half-past 766
ham 393
handbag 557
handkerchief 558
handle carefully 128
hanger 297
Happy Birthday ! 33
Happy New Year ! 34
hard-boiled eggs 389
hardware store 612
hat 559
— shop 613
have (possess, hold), 269, 304, 434, 456, 471, 474, 574 (*see also* I have)
headache 706
headlight 254
headwaiter 329

HEALTH p. 92
health certificate 112
health, to your 321
hearty appetite 364
help 95
here 43, 51, 736
here is 109
horn 255
horseback riding 517
horse race 512
HOTEL, AT THE, p. 57
hotel, 97, 261
hour 219, 757
house 459
how 86, 63
— are things 20
— are you 18
— far 162
— is 23
— long 88, 542
— many 733
— much 87, 530
hundred 810
hungry 46
hurry, in a 45

hurt 721
husband 8

I am 37, 39ff
I cannot 97, 117
I have 122, 226, 268
ice 366
icebag 656
ice cream 454, 471
identification papers 111
ILLNESS p. 92
immediately 651
in 152, 705
include 308, 359
indigestion 711
inexpensive 263
ink 632
inside 155
insurance 741
insure 741, 743
interest 484
international 226
introduce 6
iodine 665
is 23
it is 150, 162, 267, 284, 806

Jacket 560
jai alai 513
jam 384
January 789
jewelry store 614
juice 379ff
July 795
June 794

Keep the change 362
key 303
kilogram 195
kilometer 220
knife 337
know 57

Ladies' room 80
lamb 404
larger 533
last night 776
late 763
later 293, 469
laundry 683
LAUNDRY p. 90
laxative 666
leak 246
leather 642
leave (abandon) 127
leave (depart) 198, 201, 306

left (direction) 145, 113
let's go 510
let's have another 320
letter 304, 733
lettuce 421, 467
license 226
licensed guide 482
lifeboat 187
life preserver 189
light beer 318
lighter (*adj.*) 592
lighter (*n.*) 643
like (admire) 31
like (wish, prefer) 283, 302, 310, 348, 379, 449, 468, 515, 529, 631, 733, 743
lipstick 667
liqueur 317
listen 93
liter 235, 237
little, a 53, 351
liver 405
lobby 156
lobster 406, 461
local 173, 727

long-distance 728
look for 96, 261
look out 94
lose 98, 723
lost and found desk 104
lotion 695
lubricate 240
lunch 324

Magazine 628
mail 309, 734
— chute 746
mailing address 38
main street 211
make out 307
man 77
manager 302
manicure 700
map 234, 629
March 791
marinated herring 465
market 615
mashed potatoes 428
mass (relig.) 481
massage 702
mat 300
match 645
matinée 494

matter, it doesn't 72
May 793
may I 6, 30, 177, 207, 249, 537
meal 281
mean 61
measurements 539
meat 348
meat market 616
mechanic 229
medium 349
meet 17
melon 439
mend 685
men's room 79
menu 333
Merry Christmas! 35
message 304, 732
middle 153
mild 666
milk 446, 472
million 810
mine 113
mineral water 312
minimum charge 508, 751, 753
minister 478

minute 769
Miss 6
miss 100, 248
mistake 360
moderate 535
moment, a 92
Monday 782
money 99
MONTHS p. 101
monument 159
more 351
morning 771
mother 14
motor 248
movie film 646
movies 495
Mr., Mrs. 6
much, 26, 474
much, very 760
museum 489
mushroom 422
music 582
musical instrument 583
mustard 377
must I 116, 121, 179

Name 759
my name is 36
native 322
nausea 713

near 330, 163
nearest 520, 639
necktie 571
new 740
news dealer 623
newspaper 630
next 216, 781
night 775
— club 496
— letter 752
nightgown 561
nine 810
nineteen 810
ninety 810
ninety-one 810
ninety-two 810
no 66
noisy 267
north 140
not 55, 266, 342, 694
nothing 114, 118
November 799
now 244, 458
number 727, 29
NUMBERS p. 104
nylon 568

O'clock 764, 306
October 798

office 130, 131
oil 238, 373, 467
olive 419
omelet 386
one 810
one-half 753
one-way ticket 169
onion 423, 463
only 52
open 116, 202, 490
opera 497
operator 728
opposite 157
orange (color) 599
orange (fruit) 440
— juice 380
orchestra seat 503
order 355, 458, 538
other 151
others 535
outside 156
overheat 247
oyster 407

Pack 641
package 127
pain 716
painting 485

pair 555
paper 633, 637
parcel post 737
park (n.) 157
park (v.) 249
passport 110
pastry 471
— shop 617
pay 121, 544
peach 441
pea 424, 463
— soup 465
pen 634
pencil 635
pepper 372
peppers 425
per 196, 742
perhaps 67
performance 501
perfume 584
permanent wave 699
person 274
personal check 522
personal use 115
picture 585
pie 450
pillow 295
pillowcase 296
pimento 426
pink 600
pipe 644

plate 338

play 515

playing 500

plaza 208

please 25, 60, 287, 462, 736, 744

P.M. 765

policeman 106

police station 105

pork 408

postage 744

postcard 636

POST OFFICE, AT THE (Conversation) p. 96

potato 427ff

powder 668

prefer 531

prescription 651

press 687

price 535, 536

priest 476

print 759

Protestant 479

prune 382

PUBLIC NOTICES p. 106

puncture 245

purple 601

purse 98

purser 182

put 128

Quarter-past 767

quarter to 768

quickly 332

Rabbi 477

railroad station 197

raincoat 562

raining 809

rare 348

raspberry 442, 471

rate 282, 749

razor 671

— blades 672

ready 648

receipt 745

recommend 322, 459

record 586

red 602

red wine 319

regards 27

regular 734, 749

rent 225

repair 103, 690

reservation 268

reserved seat 175

residential section 136

restaurant 322

RESTAURANT p. 53

RESTAURANT, AT THE (Conversation) p. 66

rice 431

right (direction) 144, 746

right now 458

road 230, 231

ROAD SIGNS p. 112

roll 646, 647

rolls 385

room 176, 270ff

— number 305

— service 286

rouge 669

round-trip ticket 168

SALAD p. 60

Salad 357, 466

salesgirl 544

salesman 545

salt 371

sandwich 325

sanitary napkin 673
sardine 409
Saturday 787
sauce 378
sausage 410
say 63
school 158
scrambled eggs 391
sculpture 486
seasick 191
SEASONS p. 101
seat 175, 502
second class 171
sedative 674
see 28, 283, 505, 704
send 287, 733, 737, 752
September 797
serve 326, 332
service (personal) 286, 363
service (relig.) 481
service charge 359
seven 810
seventeen 810
seventy 810
sew 689
shade 592

shampoo 675, 697
shave 696
shaving cream 677
— lotion 676
sherry 313, 457
ship (v.) 543
shirt 685
shoe 103, 563
shoelace 564
shoemaker 618
shoeshine 703
shoe store 619
SHOPPING p. 74
shopping 528
SHOPPING LIST p. 76
short 694
show 135, 234, 487, 535
shower 278
shrimp 411
side 150, 151
SIGHTSEE-ING p. 69
sign 746
silver 578
silverware 587
simple 341
single room 271
sink 279
sir 746
sister 12

sit 25
six 810
sixteen 810
sixty 810
size 538
skating 518
skirt 565
sleep 717
sleeper 205
slippers 566
slowly 54, 221
smaller 534
smoke 208
smoking car 207
snapshot 649
soap 298
socks 567
soda 314
soft-boiled egg 387
sole (fish) 460
some 640
something 456, 531, 715
son 10
soon 307
sore throat 714
sorry 49, 473
so, so 22
soup 394, 395
SOUPS p. 60
south 141
souvenir 588
Spanish 63

spare tire 256
speak 50ff, 302,
482, 730
specialty 459
spell 64
spicy 344
spinach 432
spoon 339, 340,
472
SPORTS p. 72
spring (mech.)
257
spring (season)
801
stall 248
stamp 733, 735
starch 686
start 501
starter 258
station 155, 227
stationer 624
STATIONER
p. 83
stay in bed 718
steak 412
steering wheel
259
steward 183
stewed prunes
382
stockings 568
stop (n.) 216
stop (v.) 211,
223
stop (off) 177

STORES p. 82
straight ahead
154
strawberry 443,
471
street 150, 166
streetcar 208,
211
STREETCAR
p. 41
string 638
student 39
sugar 370
suit 569, 687
summer 802
Sunday 788
sunglasses 678
suntan oil 679
supper 326
sweater 570
sweet 343
swimming 519
— pool 514
Swiss cheese
471
synagogue 480

Table 330
table d'hôte
331
tailor shop 620
take (accept)
732
take (carry)
195

take 542, 733
take care of
738, 759
take it away
356
take measure-
ments 539
take snapshot
649
tank 236
tart 471, 472
tasty 460
taxi 129, 217
TAXI p. 42
tea 447, 472
teacher 40
teaspoon 339
TELEGRAM,
SENDING
A (Conver-
sation) p. 97
telephone 725
— number 29
TELEPHON-
ING p. 95
tell 95, 215
temporarily
722
ten 810
tennis 515
thanks 69, 747,
19, 470
that 149
theater 474,
498

there is 118, 285, 360
thermometer 680
these 119
things 120
think 58
third class 172
thirsty 46
thirteen 810
thirty 810
thirty-one 810
this 148
this is 122, 166, 353
thousand 810
three 810
throat 714
Thursday 785
ticket 168, 169
— office 167
TICKETS p. 36
TIME p. 99
time 193, 474
  what time is it 761
  on time 194
tip 359
tire 243, 256
to 493ff
toast 384
tobacco 644
today 778, 460
toilet paper 301

tomato 433, 467
— juice 381
tomorrow 780, 755
tonight 779, 273
too 342, 763
tooth 721, 724
toothbrush 658
toothpaste 681
toothpowder 682
topcoat 552
total 744
towel 299
town 232
toy 589
track 201
traffic light 146
train 100, 198
TRAIN p. 40
transfer 210
travel 44, 719
— agent 131
TRAVEL: GENERAL EXPRESSIONS p. 33
traveler's check 523
trousers 572
trunk 117
try on 537
tube 681

Tuesday 783
turn 139
twelve 810
twenty 810
twenty-one 810
twenty-two 810
twin beds 276
two 810

Umbrella 591
uncle 27
understand 55, 650
underwear 573
United States 733
until 4, 755
upstairs 284
use 115
USEFUL WORDS AND EXPRESSIONS p. 26
usual 750

Vacation 43
vanilla 455, 471
veal 413
vegetable 462
— soup 395
VEGETABLES p. 62

vermouth 457
very 24
very well 475
village 138
vinegar 374,
    467

Wait, 92, 224
waiter 328, 472
waiting room
    176
waitress 327
walk 164
wallet 98
want 127, 130,
    266, 273, 331,
    341, 482, 528
warm 47, 806
wash 685
watch 591
watchmaker
    621
water 239, 365
way 134, 148
on the way
    177
WEATHER
    p. 103
weather 808

Wednesday 784
week 781
welcome 70
well 24, 505,
    717
— done 350
west 143
what 82, 61,
    738
— do you wish
    89
— is 282
— is that 62
— time 326
wheel 260
when 84, 754
where 85, 737
while, a 127,
    249
whiskey 314
white 603
white wine 319,
    457
who 81
— are you 74
— is 75
— is it 292
why 83
width 541

wife 7
will you 240,
    243
window 202,
    330, 521
windshield 241
wine 319
— list 334
winter 804
wish 5
with 366
within 757
without 367
woman 78
word 61, 748
wrapping
    paper 637
write 59
writing paper
    633

Yellow 604
yes 65
yesterday 777
you 19
YOURSELF
    p. 22

Zipper 690